MW01520343

KINGDOM
FOUNDATIONS
for
Supernatural Living

Ian Wilkinson

Copyright © 2012—Ian Wilkinson

All rights reserved. This book is protected under the copyright laws. This book may not be copied or reprinted for commercial gain or profit. The use of short quotations or occasional page copying for personal or group study is permitted and encouraged. Permission will be granted upon request. Unless otherwise identified, Scripture quotations are from the New King James Version. Copyright © 1982 by Thomas Nelson Inc. Used with permission. All rights reserved. Scripture marked NIV are from the Holy Bible, New International Version ®, copyright 1973, 1978, 1984, 2010, International Bible society. Used with permission of Zondervan. All rights reserved. Scripture marked NLT are from Scripture quotations marked KJV are taken from the King James Version of the Bible, whose copyright ran out centuries ago. Its text is now in the public domain. The Holy Bible, New Living Translation, copyright 1996, 2004. Used by permission of Tyndale House Publishers, Wheaton, Illinois 60189. All rights reserved. All emphasis within Scripture is the author's own.

Please note that Destiny Image Europe's publishing style capitalizes certain pronouns in Scripture that refer to the Father, Son, and Holy Spirit, and may differ from some publishers' styles. Take note that the name satan and related names are not capitalized. We choose not to acknowledge him, even to the point of violating grammatical rules.

DESTINY IMAGE™ EUROPE srl
Via Maiella, 1
66020 San Giovanni Teatino (Ch) – Italy

"Changing the World, One Book at a Time."™

This book and all other Destiny Image™ Europe and Evangelista Media™ books are available at Christian bookstores and distributors worldwide.

To order products, or for any other correspondence:

EVANGELISTA MEDIA™
Via della Scafa 29/14
65013 Città Sant'Angelo (Pe), Italy
Tel. +39 085 4716623
Fax: +39 085 9090113

Email: info@evangelistamedia.com
Or reach us on the Internet: www.evangelistamedia.com

ISBN 13: 978-88-96727-49-2
ISBN 13 Ebook: 978-88-96727-51-5

For Worldwide Distribution, Printed in Canada
1 2 3 4 5 / 16 15 14 13 12

Dedication

This book is dedicated to two disciples of the Lord Jesus. I dedicate Part I to Dr. Keith Hazell of Lethbridge, Alberta. He is an incredible prophet and teacher of God who prayed for me to be baptized in the Holy Spirit during the Jesus People Movement 40 years ago and was my mentor for those first few years. He demonstrated a vibrant Christianity that exuded the joy of the life lived before God. His ability to prophesy is so accurate and detailed—it is almost beyond supernatural.

I dedicate Part II of this book to the memory of a beloved brother, Reverend James Thomas of Calgary, Alberta, who is now with the Lord. He was a big man with an enormous spirit and a true, *huios* (mature) son of God. He read my teachings about the kingdom of God and insisted that I teach kingdom foundations in the three seminaries where he served as Dean of Faculty.

Contents

Foreword

I have known Ian Wilkinson for nearly four decades. During that time, Ian has been a friend and a mentor. I can remember him coming to my door and confirming a word to me to get into the ministry. In my early life as a pastor, Ian would routinely call me and encourage me with his insights and words of wisdom.

Years later, when we were going through a rough time in the pastorate, Ian was there for us, over and over again, watching over us with care.

He has always held a fascination for me, as he would enthusiastically share with us his latest pondering about Scripture and what he found within the pages of the Bible. His take on certain doctrines would always be inspiring and often times had me contemplating his version of his newfound discovery.

Ian is succinct and blunt. Even if it was going to hurt to hear what he was going to say, he would confront any issue and speak in love. That's what friends do. To quote Charles Kingsley: *A blessed thing it is for any man or woman to have a friend; one human soul whom we can trust utterly; who knows the best and the worst of us, and who loves us in spite of all our faults; who will speak the honest truth to us, while the world flatters us to our face, and laughs at us behind our back.*

Ian's pursuit to understand the kingdom of God fits completely with who he is. He is on a constant errand to find out just what God meant when He gave us His blueprint for life—the Bible.

Peter McManus, Editorial Director
City Light News
Calgary, Alberta, Canada
www.calgarychristian.com

Part I

Becoming Huios (Becoming Spirit-Led)

For as many as are governed by the Spirit of God,
they are the sons [huios] *of God (Romans 8:14).*
(*huios* – Greek; mature son, having the nature of his Father)

The Spirit itself testifies with our spirit, that we are
the children [teknon] *of God (Romans 8:16).*
(*teknon* – Greek; legal offspring)

The creation waits in eager expectation for the sons
[huios] *of God to be revealed (Romans 8:19 NIV).*

Chapter One

Creation Is Waiting

For the earnest expectation of the creation eagerly waits for the revealing of the sons of God (Romans 8:19).

When you decide to build a house, the first thing you must do is have a picture or a vision of what it is you want. Then once you have a blueprint, you need to build the proper foundation for the house. The first part of *Kingdom Foundations for Supernatural Living* presents an image of what you could become. Part II explains the foundation you will need to accomplish that goal. I believe that supernatural living is the birthright of those believers in the Lord Jesus who have decided to make the effort to mature spiritually.

A Christian with a good understanding of the kingdom of God can step forward into the supernatural with confidence. Jesus warns in Matthew 7:22 that there will be people who operate supernaturally—but improperly, without authorization. This means it is not enough to operate supernaturally, we must do so properly, which is why we need a good foundation. The Bible encourages us to get wisdom and get understanding even though it may cost all we have.

I have discovered the benefit of having good kingdom theology and using it as a system for evaluating teaching I hear. It also helps me organize my thoughts. People ask me, "How do you remember all this stuff?" Well, it's because the kingdom foundation I have learned provides me with an index, or organizational system, to structure my thinking. This valuable kingdom theology is detailed in Part II.

Huios

The biblical word for mature believer is the Greek word *huios*. The reason I choose to use the Greek word rather than the English word "son" is because by defining it for you, it can remain sharp and clear without the complications of connotations. If I used the English "son," you would possibly have ideas about it and baggage that would interfere with absorbing my intentions. For example, in this book "son" or *huios* is not gender specific. A *huios* is a believer—male or female—who is spiritually mature enough to operate supernaturally and lawfully. Jesus is the *Huios* of God, the mature Son, who reflects the nature of the Father. He said, "If you have seen Me, you have seen the Father" (John 14:9).

After exploring the possibility of becoming a *huios* in Part I, our focus turns toward the proper foundations needed to adjust our thinking so that we can accomplish our goal. In other words, to change our current theology into kingdom-centered theology. The kingdom foundation will enable us to move forward spiritually.

This book is written to assist people who want to learn how to be led of the Spirit. You may have heard that God is moving. People are experiencing healings, signs, and wonders. Maybe you want more of God. Maybe you want to move supernaturally. All of creation is ready and waiting to see dynamic Christianity. People are waiting for the revealing of the sons of God. By that, I do not mean some sect or cult. I mean mature followers of Christ who have learned to hear and obey the Holy Spirit and who actually heal the sick and open blind eyes. I mean believers who, like Jesus, have the confidence to do what they hear the Spirit say to do.

Church Life

For some of us who have been Christians for many years, the main component of our Christian life has been attending church. Churches have provided us with important information, encouragement, and opportunities. But for some of us, perhaps more than some, the current system of doing church has limited our involvement. There are a growing number of dedicated born-again, eldership-level believers who have left conventional churches. Many have started house churches. Many want more than what was expected at conventional services.

Maybe you attend a good church and you're happy there. That's good. I would not want to pull you away from that. Not everyone is having that experience, though. Let's be real. Bottom line for many churches—what they want most from you is your attendance. As a retired pastor, I know of what I speak. I still think attendance is important. After attendance, it is your financial contribution that is important. It could be they expect you to be at prayer meetings as well. Some churches encourage outreach. Perhaps they really want your participation as an usher or a parking lot attendant or a Sunday school teacher. But there are a few very important components of spirituality that are missing.

These are generalities, but I venture to say that few church leaders encourage you, for example, to become Spirit-led. Few want you to pray about where to donate your money or God's tithe this month. How many allow the Holy Spirit to administrate activities? You are expected to listen to a sermon, not be one. You are not welcome to give verbal contributions or insights during a sermon or to challenge the status quo. You may be called to be a prophet or an apostle, but the leadership is not equipped to help launch you into ministry. Does your church have a mission statement to make you a mature Christ-led son (*huios*) of God able to heal all who are oppressed of the devil? Maybe not, but God does.

This book is not a novel. It is more of a learning tool. I address some theological issues and issues of tradition that interfere with the process of spiritual maturity. I write about things that prevent us becoming carbon copies of Jesus, like the traditions of men that make the Word of God of no effect. We are comfortable sitting in special buildings designed to separate "ministers" from audiences. We are content to have paid performers entertain us with inspired music and rhetoric. We pay missionaries to reach the lost, for staff members to pray for the sick, and for facilities to house our Christian activities.

There are instances of churches that are doing extraordinary things; but in general, we are an isolated, ineffective sub-culture that is not changing or impacting our world. We need to be involved directly with people in the community—hearing their ideas, challenging their unbelief, and demonstrating the power of God's kingdom.

Doing Good

Jesus had no buildings or building funds. He had no methods of mass communication. He simply returned from the wilderness one day empowered by the Holy Spirit and went about doing good—healing sick people and casting out demons. When He demonstrated the power of the Holy Spirit, He said the kingdom of God is among you. Soon word-of-mouth advertising made it all but impossible for Him to enter a town unnoticed. The secret of His success is that He learned to hear what the Spirit was asking Him to do, and He did it with the power the Spirit provided. He taught out in the streets. He modeled what He did to His disciples so they could do the same.

We are falling a wee bit short of doing things like Peter and Paul. We need to mature spiritually. It's time for *teknons* (born-again believers) to grow up into *huios*. This requires a change in our thinking, which will in turn produce a change in our actions. We need to start seeing the kingdom point of view. This book brings you a kingdom perspective.

Is it possible to be governed by the Spirit? I believe so. Do you?

The *Huios* of God

I believe it is important to delve more deeply into the terms used throughout, which present a special view of our relationship with our heavenly Father. A *huios* (pronounced wee-ohs) is a mature son who reflects the nature of his father. Jesus is the *Huios* of God. When we are born again, we become "the legal offspring" or *teknon* of God, but we do not reflect His nature immediately. It takes discipleship and growth. In order to be truly called *huios*, we must be led or governed by the Holy Spirit. It is not enough to be filled with the Spirit, we must be ruled by the Spirit as well. As a *huios* we think and act like Jesus. A mature son is ready to take on the family business. Jesus said He must be about His Father's business (see Luke 2:49).

So while we define *huios* as a mature son who reflects the nature of the Father or one who is led of the Spirit, we describe a *huios* as one who is able to do both the will of God (obedience) and the works of God as in healing the sick, raising the dead, opening blind eyes, etc. The ability to do signs and wonders in and of itself does not indicate the depth of a *huios's* maturity but it is a vital component of being a *huios* to which I hope we all aspire. We will hopefully develop a Spirit-led walk where we learn to do the will and the works of God, for this is what it means to be a *huios*.

Creation is not waiting for the *teknons* to be revealed. Creation is not impressed with *teknons*. Creation, I believe, is quite frankly bored with *teknons*. Creation is waiting for those who are led by the Spirit to stand up. All of creation is eagerly waiting for mature disciples of Jesus to show up and heal the sick, cast out demons, turn water into wine, perform miracles, and work signs and wonders out in the streets and in the community—just like the original *Huios* did. The question is, "Are you going to one of them?"

Teknons Are Us

Most every born-again Christian you meet is a *teknon*. To be a *teknon* is a good thing. It means that you are adopted into the family of God. Some people define born again to mean "saved." Saved to them inevitably means not going to hell. Point in fact, Jesus did not actually save us from hell, per se. He saved us from sin. We are also saved from the consequences of sin, one being an eternity in hell.

In the context of the kingdom of God, born again means "under new management." It means we are no longer governed by sin, which leads to death and hell. We are now officially under the government of the Holy Spirit. We who were slaves to sin have become slaves of righteousness. At least, we are *supposed* to be under new management if we are born again. Becoming a *huios* is the process of turning the legal opportunity, or possibility of being governed by the Spirit, into a daily functioning reality.

Most of us who are evangelicals are not well-versed in the kingdom meaning of born again. Evangelicals comprise the segment of Christians we most often associate with being Bible-believing, born-again, evangelize-the-world type of Christians. They include Baptists, Pentecostals, Charismatics, and an assortment of others. In an attempt to add some clarity, I have chosen to call Baptists and the like, Evangelicals with a capital E and all Bible-believing, born-again, evangelize-the-world Christians as evangelicals with a small e.

Though many evangelicals have been baptized in the Spirit, the term Evangelicals is often used for those Bible believers who have not. It can be confusing. Spirit-filled evangelicals, in general, such as Pentecostals or Full Gospels often do not have "Pentecostal" theology. They have what is essentially Baptist theology with an addendum about the Holy Spirit. They have no fully integrated Spirit-based theology, which is unfortunate, because one is sorely needed.

I was teaching an evening class at a Pentecostal seminary in Ternopil, Ukraine. Most of the class was made up of young people preparing for the ministry. The son of the local Baptist minister was attending. I was teaching an integrated theology in which the Holy Spirit was woven into the whole, rather than added to Baptist theology. Before the first evening of teaching about the baptism of the Holy Spirit, the Baptist minister's son spoke to me. He was very concerned, because he was a Baptist and did not believe as I did regarding the Holy Spirit. He was wondering if he answered the exam questions according to what he personally believed as opposed to what I taught, would he be marked down for it. I replied in typical professor fashion that he would be tested for his ability to regurgitate course content. He seemed resigned to that. So I began the first of two four-hour sessions on the Holy Spirit.

At the end of the first evening, the young Baptist came up to me quite excited and told me that he now believed halfway between what he used to believe and what I believe. At the end of the second four-hour session, he told me that he believed as I do. All it took was some good theology, and he was convinced. We don't have to be embarrassed about good Holy Spirit theology. But we do have to be embarrassed about disjointed, Evangelical theology with a patch work of Holy Spirit addendums. Unfortunately most Spirit-filled believers have evangelical theology with the experience of speaking in tongues added. So for my purposes, I classify Pentecostals, Full Gospels, Charismatics, etc. with evangelicals because they have the same basic theology.

The other main category in Christianity is traditional or liturgical and includes Roman Catholic, High Anglican, Eastern Orthodox, etc. Some classify these into three groupings: Traditional, Evangelical and Spirit-filled. In this case the Evangelicals would be groups like the Baptists, but not include Pentecostals. Some denominations, like the Anglicans, have all three groups. There are Traditional Anglicans, Evangelical Anglicans, and Spirit-filled Anglicans.

As mentioned previously, most evangelicals were not taught the kingdom meaning of born again. We were, in fact, taught the concept of justification. Justification means having our sins removed, which effectively gets us right with God. It means that we are righteous before God. Righteousness can mean either right-standing or right-living. Right-standing is associated with justification, and right-living is associated with sanctification. When we were born again, according to an evangelical point of view, we were justified. We were saved. They are seen as synonymous.

Justification by faith is the wonderful truth restored by Martin Luther. It is the central tenet of the Protestant faith. We understand it to mean that the work of Jesus on the cross is what saved us—not our own works. Or in the case of the medieval church, it is faith, not paying indulgences to the church, that saves us. When we place our full confidence or faith in the sacrifice of Jesus and the blood He shed to remove our sins, then we are made right with God. We, in effect, accept what God did to reconcile us to Himself and we don't try to justify ourselves with religious good works.

That if you confess with your mouth the Lord Jesus and believe in your heart that God has raised Him from the dead, you will be saved (Romans 10:9).

Method One: Justification

Justification can be achieved in one of two ways. The first method is to do all the commands of God—lead a sinless life. It can mean to follow the teachings of Moses to the letter: "Then it will be righteousness for us, if we are careful to observe all these commandments before the LORD our God, as He has commanded us" (Deut. 6:25). This method, though it has some appeal, has been shown irrefutably to be impossible because all have sinned and fall short (see Rom. 3:23).

The Rich Young Ruler Story

Now as He [Jesus] *was going out on the road, one came running, knelt before Him, and asked Him, "Good Teacher, what shall I do that I may inherit eternal life?" So Jesus said to him, "Why do you call Me good? No one is good but One, that is, God. You know the commandments: 'Do not commit adultery,' 'Do not murder,' 'Do not steal,' 'Do not bear false witness,' 'Do not defraud,' 'Honor your father and your mother.'" And he answered and said to Him, "Teacher, all these things I have kept from my youth." Then Jesus, looking at him, loved him, and said to him, "One thing you lack: Go your way, sell whatever you have and give to the poor, and you will have treasure in heaven; and come, take up the cross, and follow Me." But he was sad at this word, and went away sorrowful, for he had great possessions* (Mark 10:17-22).

It might seem that this passage is saying that the rich man was obedient to the commands of God. Jesus looked at him, loved him, and spoke gently. To us it looks like Jesus did not correct him, so we deduce the young man spoke the truth, but think again. "For whom the Lord *loves* He corrects, just as a father the son in whom he delights" (Prov. 3:12). So Jesus is going to correct him. Remember, all have sinned. What the young ruler said was impossible, and Jesus knew it. When Jesus said "one thing you lack," He wasn't adding something new to the Ten Commandments. He was starting at the first commandment. "You shall have no other gods before Me" (Exod. 20:3). Then, "You cannot serve God and mammon" (Matt. 6:24). He was gently pointing out that the young ruler hadn't even kept the first of the Ten Commandments.

Jesus did love this man, but that doesn't mean that Jesus approved of all the man said. After Adam sinned, God barred humankind access to the tree of life. God still loved man. God has always loved man and always will. *Nothing can separate us from the love of God.* But dear loved one, if you die in sin, you will burn for eternity. Hell is full of people God loves. His love alone cannot save you. It motivates Him to provide a solution for sin, but you and I must apply that solution by faith for it to be effective. We are clearly told in the New Testament that we can only be justified by faith. So method one is useless.

Purpose of the Law

The law of God, or the law of Moses, actually refers to the "teaching" of God that He gave to Moses. Law or *nomos* means teaching and includes the commands of God. (Antinomian means against the law or without the law.) Law is a word that has many denotations including principle and regulation, so it is important to distinguish and clarify its meaning. When I was a school teacher many years ago, we had a saying, "We don't hate school just the principle (principal) of the thing." This might not be humorous in some countries where they use the term "head" instead of principal. Head is the same word used for toilet on a ship. Words can have such diverse and interesting denotations and connotations. The first five books of the Bible are referred to as the law. They serve as the vital foundation for the rest of the Word of God and provide the necessary criteria for establishing that Yeshua, or Jesus, is indeed the Messiah.

The law of God is very important; but in the context of justification, it is almost useless. It does define sin. It does reveal sin. It does *not* remove sin. The law is like a mirror. You look in the mirror and perhaps you see a smudge of chocolate on your cheek. The mirror will not remove the chocolate, it just reveals the problem. So you might use a damp cloth or soap and water to remove the smudge. It is the same with sin. Only the blood of Jesus washes away sin. The law is good because it shows us our need to be clean, and the blood is good because it washes us. Both are gifts from God.

As you read the Epistles, you will find what could be seen as conflicting statements about the law. In one place it states that the law is good and that the law is spiritual. In another place you can read that the law is useless or that we died to the law. It can be quite confusing. Not only do we have what seems like conflicting statements in the text, but also we have the difficulties of translation from the Greek.

The New International Version of the New Testament translates Ephesians 2:15 [speaking of Jesus making peace] by abolishing in His flesh, "the law with its commandments and regulations." So reading it this way, it is saying that the law is abolished, end of story; or so it would seem. We also read that Jesus said in Matthew 5:17, "Do not think that I came to destroy the law...but to fulfill." It seems to be a contradiction! The New King James Version more correctly translates the passage in Ephesians 2:15 as He made peace by abolishing in His flesh *the enmity* of the law. The enmity of the law was the division between Greek and Jew caused by the law. So, Jesus abolished the division between Jew and Gentile not the law. The word used for fulfill in this passage means to make replete or to fill to the brim, not to fulfill as a contract.

It will help you to know that when the context of the passage is justification, then the law is spoken of in a negative sense because it is useless for justification. So if you are reading a passage where the law is spoken of as "bad," check the context, and you will find it to be justification. In other contexts, the law will be spoken of in positive way. The law is our school master that brings us to Christ. That's a good thing. The law is what convicts us that we need a Savior.

John 1:16-17 tells us that "of His fullness we have received grace gift after grace gift for because through Moses the law was given, grace and truth through Jesus Christ became" (from Greek transliteration). The original Greek brings out the cause and effect better than modern translations. Both the law and Jesus are grace gifts. God authored the law and He likes it, but it is useless for removing chocolate smudges from your face or sin from your heart. So to review, the law is not effective at removing sins; or in other words, it cannot justify us before God. Let's move to the second method of being justified.

Method Two: Call on the Name of the Lord

The second method is to call on the name of the Lord: "if you confess with your mouth the Lord Jesus and believe in your heart that God has raised him from the dead, you will be saved" (Rom. 10:9). "For Christ is the end of the law for righteousness [justification] to everyone who believes" (Rom. 10:4). It turns out that this second method is really the *only* method. Before expanding on this method of justification, we will in the next section look at the new birth from a kingdom perspective. This kingdom perspective of the new birth is developed more fully in Part II.

Just before heading into the new birth, let's lock down some ideas about the law. This subject can be confusing. First of all, God authored the law. Second, Jesus upheld it. But it cannot justify us before God because it does not have the power to do so. In the context of salvation other than revealing what sin is and our need for salvation, the law cannot help us. Attempts to be saved by obeying the law are counterproductive; so in many evangelical circles, the law is seen as detrimental not only to the process of justification but also to the process of Christian living.

Our Protestant point of view does not always perfectly reflect the point of view of the early church. It must be remembered that they were still very Jewish; but in the centuries after the early church, the Roman Catholics separated from the Jews, and then the Protestants separated from the Catholics. It is exciting to realize that there are many Messianic (Jews who believe that Yeshua is the Son of God) churches around today that were virtually unheard of 40 years ago when I first got saved. So it might be good to note Paul's ideas and attitudes concerning the law. He said things like: The law is good when used lawfully. The law is spiritual. The law was our schoolmaster (tutor). Faith upholds the law. Loves fulfills the law. He wrote the following:

But we know that the law is good if one uses it lawfully (1 Timothy 1:8).

For we know that the law is spiritual, but I am carnal, sold under sin (Romans 7:14).

Because the carnal mind is enmity against God; for it is not subject to the law of God, nor indeed can be (Romans 8:7).

Therefore the law was our tutor to bring us to Christ, that we might be justified by faith (Galatians 3:24).

Do we then make **void** *the law through faith? Certainly not! On the contrary, we* **establish** *the law* (Romans 3:31).

Love does no harm to a neighbor; therefore love is the fulfilment of the law (Romans 13:10).

And remember what Jesus Himself said about the law:

For assuredly, I say to you, till heaven and earth pass away, one jot or one tittle will by no means pass from the law till all is fulfilled. Whoever therefore breaks one of the least of these commandments, and teaches men so, shall be called least in the kingdom of heaven; but whoever does and teaches them, he shall be called great in the kingdom of heaven (Matthew 5:18-19).

You may have noticed that Heaven and earth have not yet passed away; and that in the context of the kingdom, the law has validity. So although from a correct evangelical perspective of salvation we do not keep the law in order to get saved, we find that in the context of kingdom living, the law has some value. Principally, the law has value since the law is the teaching contained in the first five books of the Bible. We know that the law has no value at removing sin, and that our sins are removed through faith in the finished work of Jesus. The sacrificial laws or portion of the law dealing with the sacrifices for sin are obsolete. The moral law, on the other hand, is still very much intact.

Since the law is spiritual, it has importance for us who want to be Spirit-led. Paul says he serves the law with his mind, "So then, with the mind *I myself serve the law of God*, but with the flesh the law of sin" (Rom. 7:25). **It is carnal not to serve the law of God.** Jesus said in Matthew 7:23, to certain men that were doing supernatural works, that they were practicing **lawlessness**. We don't want to practice law-lessness. There is a way to serve the law without being legalistic. The early church did it. So we see that the early church may have had a different outlook toward the law than modern-day evangelicals do, but let us go on and look at the new birth.

The New Birth

I was born again 40 years ago in a Pentecostal church that had embraced the hippie-like Jesus People. It was the late 1960s-early '70s. God was moving, and thousands of young people were getting saved. Back in those days, the "word" was Acts 2:38—repent and be baptized and you will receive the gift of the Holy Spirit. In the first three years of the move of God in that church, we saw more than a thousand people water baptized. We had more than 200 young people loving on Jesus in our version of college and careers.

> *Then Peter said to them, "Repent, and let every one of you be baptized in the name of Jesus Christ for the remission of sins; and you shall receive the gift of the Holy Spirit"* (Acts 2:38).

At my first exposure to these Jesus People, I resisted going forward during the altar call. I knew one of the members of the church because he worked at the same office I did. His name was Keith Hazell and he was strange. We called him "Hazell nut" at the office. Anyway, after hearing the gospel I went home, and God began to convict me not of sin but of truth. I knelt beside my bed that night and prayed, though I felt a bit like an idiot doing it. I said, "God if You are real and Jesus is really who these people say He is, I will follow Him." Then I stood up. I was lighter. It was like a heavy backpack had been removed from my shoulders.

The next night I returned to the Jesus People church. They were having meetings all the time back then. The preacher asked whoever would like the Holy Spirit to come forward. So I went forward. I was met at the altar by Hazell nut himself. Keith said to raise my hands and then he prayed. I felt electricity flow through my hands and arms into my chest and I burst out speaking in some weird language. I think the term for that is called being baptized in the Holy

Ghost. Later that same night, I was water baptized. I had experienced being initiated into the kingdom of God, but it wasn't until years later that I fully understood the process. David Pawson has written a choice book called *The Normal Christian Birth* that really helped me.

So let's talk about the first steps into the kingdom of God called the new birth. This is dealt with in greater depth in Part II, Kingdom Foundations.

Your proper initiation into the kingdom of God, or the government of God, begins with hearing or reading testimony to the reality of God and His laws and your need to be saved from sin and hell. This prepares you for repentance, which simply means a change of thinking. The Greek word *metanoia* focuses on the change of mind aspect of repentance, but the Hebrew concept makes it clear that the change of mind produces a change of action as well. Repentance is something that is ongoing for the growing Christian; but the greatest repentance is when we no longer see Jesus as just a historical figure or as a curse word, but as Lord Creator. You see Jesus for who He really is, which leads to the next step—believing that He is Lord.

When a person believes in Jesus as Lord, it is not the same as believing that someone exists or existed. I believe that Hitler existed, but I do not place my confidence or trust in him as I do in Jesus. So seeing, or being convinced, that Jesus is Lord and confessing with your mouth that He is Lord is more than just affirming your belief in His existence. It is adjusting your whole life to conform with the new paradigm in which you have a Ruler.

John's Gospel chapter 3 speaks of seeing and then entering the kingdom, or government, of God. When you repent of your sins of neglecting and disobeying God and believe that Jesus is Lord, you "see" the kingdom. When you see the King, you see the kingdom. The kingdom of God equals the lordship of Yeshua.

The next step is to enter that kingdom. You do that by dying to your old way of life and then receiving power to live in a new way. As a person taking initial steps toward God's government, you follow His command to be baptized or immersed in water. This identifies you with the death and burial of Jesus and is symbolic of the crossing of the Red Sea. The death of Jesus as the Passover Lamb produced the sacrifice, or the blood, that cleanses us from sin. The water removes sin's control. Think of Egypt's armies as the power of sin sent to force you back under sin's control. They were destroyed in the Red Sea. Water baptism cuts you off from sin's control, because you die with Christ. Sin has no control over a dead person (see Rom. 6:4-6).

As you come up out of the water, you identify with His resurrection from the dead. God fills you with the Holy Spirit. He breathes new life into a dead person. The Holy Spirit not only comes as a new and abiding power source, He also comes to govern and guide you into all truth. You have entered the kingdom of God.

The kingdom of God is the realm ruled by Christ. It is a domain in which you are legally free of enslavement to sin and the fear of man. You entered it by acknowledging that Jesus, Yeshua, is Lord, Yahweh. You are now back in Eden with access to the tree of life. You can now learn to rule and reign in this life. You enter this kingdom realm by coming under new management in a four-step process called the new birth. You are born again, a *teknon*, a child of God. You are a babe. Your whole life is before you. As a child, you need to be fed and discipled. You can learn the Word of God. You have the possibility of hearing and obeying the Spirit. You can become ruled by Christ.

Let's review what's been presented so far:

To be born again means to come under new management. It is four-step process of seeing and then entering the kingdom or government of God.

Seeing

Step 1. Repentance.

Step 2. Faith or believing that Jesus is Lord.

Entering

Step 3. Immersion in water.

Step 4. Baptism of the Holy Spirit.

This process is the new birth. The result: you become a *teknon*, a new-born legitimate child of God who is in desperate need of food, discipline, and reprogramming or transforming of your mind. This experience is a gateway into a life of learning to mature into a *huios* of God. You are now in the kingdom of God.

From God's point of view, sending Jesus to die on the cross was for the purpose of reconciling man to Himself. Man had sinned and so fellowship with God was adversely affected. Sin brought separation and death. How had man sinned in the first place? He sinned when he did the one thing he was instructed not to do. By disobedience, Adam and Eve not only broke the command of God, but they did damage to their relationship with Him by denying God's nature. They denied God's right to rule their lives. The only way a relationship can be reconciled is when both parties participate.

God did His part by providing a payment or sacrifice to eliminate the debt man incurred through disobedience. But man must do his part as well. Man must acknowledge that he has sinned against God; and in order to put things right, he must also acknowledge God's inherent right to rule over him. That is why when we first return to God we must confess that He is Lord. Note: We are not commanded in Scripture to confess that He is Savior in order to be saved but to confess that He is Lord. Confession is made unto salvation.

Confession is essential because it shows that *we know* that He is Lord and *are prepared* to have a relationship *on that basis*. This is extremely vital. Sometimes, perhaps most times, when confession is made unto salvation, the new convert has no idea that he or she is agreeing to come under new government. The person has no idea that the new relationship with God is on the basis that Jesus gets to be Lord and Master. Converts just think that Jesus is saving them from hell. This is why, in my opinion, the fallout rate is so high in modern-day evangelism. I've read that a large percentage of new converts fail to remain Christians for more than a year. This fact holds true for crusades and outreaches—both Baptist and Pentecostal. Ray Comfort writes in *Hell's Best Keep Secret* that 96 percent of new converts fall away in the first year. They fall away because they were not prepared to have a relationship with Jesus or a restored relationship with God on the basis of lordship.

Jesus died for our sins not only to save us from death, not only to impart life, but to restore what man had before the Fall. Man lived in paradise. Man walked with God. Things were good. Man knew that God was Lord and did what God told him to do. Man was a servant.

Servants

*And having been perfected, He [Yeshua] became the author of eternal salvation to all **who obey Him*** (Hebrews 5:9)

The Lord God planted a garden eastward in Eden, and there He put the man whom He had formed. And out of the ground the Lord God made every tree grow that is pleasant to the sight and good for food. The tree of life was also in the midst of the garden, and the tree of the knowledge of good and evil. Then the Lord God took the man and put him in the garden of Eden to tend and keep it (Genesis 2:8-9,15).

We see from the language used in the Genesis passage that Adam, the son of God, basically only knew *one* life in the Garden, that of a servant. Even though he was technically a son, he lived like a servant. Jesus, the Son of God, also lived like a servant. Romans 14 mentions we serve Christ, "For the kingdom of God is not eating and drinking, but righteousness and peace and joy in the Holy Spirit. For he who serves Christ in these things is acceptable to God and approved by men" (Rom. 14:17-18). This comes as a bit of a surprise to evangelical thinking. Somehow our culture has blinded us to the truth expressed in Romans chapter 1. It is expressed repeatedly in the New Testament. I include a few verses to illustrate.

*Paul, a **bondservant** of Jesus Christ, called to be an apostle, separated to the gospel of God which He promised before through His prophets in the Holy Scriptures, concerning His Son Jesus Christ our Lord, who was born of the seed of David according to the flesh, and declared to be the Son of God with power according to the Spirit of holiness, by the resurrection from the dead. Through Him we have received grace and apostleship **for obedience to the faith** among all nations for His name* (Romans 1:1-5).

Then the word of God spread, and the number of the disciples multiplied greatly in Jerusalem, and a great many of the priests were obedient to the faith (Acts 6:7).

When I express the idea that we are called to be servants it can meet with resistance. We have been taught that we *cannot* obey the law so often that obedience to God is out of the question. One might think that I am promoting legalism, saying you must obey God in order to be saved. I am not. I am saying that you must obey God now that you are saved. We have also been taught that born again means we are children not servants of God. In truth, we are both. God is our Father, just like He was Adam's Father and Jesus' Father. Jesus is the Son of God and the Servant of God. The disciples certainly saw themselves as servants. They introduced themselves in the Epistles as bondservants not sons. That is significant.

*"For truly against Your **holy Servant Jesus**, whom You anointed, both Herod and Pontius Pilate, with the Gentiles and the people of Israel, were gathered together to do whatever Your hand and Your purpose determined before to be done. Now, Lord, look on their threats, and grant to **Your servants** that with all boldness they may speak Your word, by stretching out Your hand to heal, and that signs and wonders may be done through the name of Your holy Servant Jesus." And when they had prayed, the place where they were assembled together was shaken; and they were all filled with the Holy Spirit, and they spoke the word of God with boldness* (Acts 4:27-31).

*The Revelation of Jesus Christ, which God gave Him to show His **servants**—things which must shortly take place. And He sent and signified it by His angel to **His servant** John* (Revelation 1:1).

*Simon Peter, a **bondservant** and apostle of Jesus Christ...* (2 Peter 1:1).

Bondservant is from the Greek *doulos. Doulos* means a slave or bondservant, one who has subjugated his will to another's. A *doulos* does the will of the Father. The apostles were therefore calling themselves slaves. Jesus said to be great in the kingdom you must be a slave of all (see Matt. 20:26-27).

Three Types of Servants

There are three types of servants mentioned in Scripture, the slave, the servant, and the steward. A steward was more of a manager than a field hand. He would oversee the estate or the business affairs of the master. Joseph was promoted by Potiphar to be overseer of his whole household. Though Joseph was a slave, he was honored by his master and given much authority. This is a picture of the servant that Adam was called to be. Humankind was called to manage the estate and given authority. We are called to rule and reign in Christ in very much the same way.

After the Hebrews left Egypt and entered Canaan, being a slave was commonly a temporary position. They were released in the Year of Release, which came every seven years. If they choose not to leave their master's service, they could become slaves for life in a ceremony that involved piercing the ear. If they chose to stay with the master, they prospered with the master. Please note in the following Scripture passage that when slaves were released, they were to be sent away with wealth just like when they left Egypt. When they left Egypt, they plundered the Egyptians of gold, silver, and fine clothing. They left Egypt wealthy.

Often we can read and reread the Scriptures and still miss important truths. It is almost as if we are blind to certain things. The idea that the former slaves left Egypt with wealth often eludes people. To escape physical slavery to become victims of economic tyranny is no salvation. God's concept of salvation includes freedom from slavery, poverty, and sickness. I think it mentions three times in the Exodus account that the Jews would plunder the Egyptians.

I was teaching on this in Malawi, Africa, and my good friend, retired school principal and pastor Harry Alufazema, was translating for me at a pastor's seminar. He told me that he had read Exodus many times and had never seen this. They have such poverty in Malawi that a poverty mentality is most likely affecting the church there.

Here in North America we can be blind to concepts like being a servant of the Lord. It is true of Americans and even us Canadians. We can read and reread the Scriptures and miss the concept. When

Jesus says that He who would be great must be a slave, we don't honestly know what to do with it. We have no personal experience with the concept. Speaking of *slaves*, we return to our look at the temporary slaves in the Promised Land.

> *If your brother, a Hebrew man, or a Hebrew woman, is sold to you and serves you six years, then in the seventh year you shall let him go free from you. And when you send him away free from you, **you shall not let him go away empty-handed;** you shall supply him **liberally** from your flock, from your threshing floor, and from your winepress. From what the Lord your God has blessed you with, you shall give to him. You shall remember that you were a slave in the land of Egypt, and the Lord your God redeemed you; therefore I command you this thing today. And if it happens that he says to you, "I will not go away from you," because he loves you and your house, **since he prospers with you,** then you shall take an awl and thrust it through his ear to the door, and he shall be your servant forever. Also to your female servant you shall do likewise* (Deuteronomy 15:12-17).

Our image of slavery is mostly formed by stories we have heard of the mistreatment of the Blacks more than a century ago in the southern United States. We see a field hand being whipped and beaten and forced to work through the heat of the day. We see a lifetime of poverty and a cry for freedom from cruel bondage. This is not the same picture we see in Deuteronomy 15. Here we see a slave who loves his master and prospers with his master. This is a truer picture of the bondservant we are called to be.

Hopefully these two pictures—Joseph in Potiphar's house and the teaching of Moses from Deuteronomy 15—serve as examples of the type of position a slave or servant or steward has in God's economy. Another example would be Abraham's servant who was sent to get a wife for Isaac. These in turn help us to interpret stories told by the Lord such as the one in Luke 12:41-48, "Who then is that faithful and wise steward, whom his master will make ruler over his household...."

Did you ever consider how many of the parables center on the theme of servants and masters? Servants or masters are mentioned

50 times in the Gospel of Matthew alone. It is a predominant theme in the parables. So whether or not we get the picture, it is pretty clear that God holds a picture in His mind that He is master and we are servants. So when you were born again, you might have thought only in terms of being safe from hell, but God was thinking in terms of His lordship.

It's not that God was trying to enslave humankind or pamper Himself with thousands of servants. It's that at the core of God's nature, He really and truly is LORD. He wants us to know Him intimately for who He truly is (see Heb. 8:11). Recognizing that truth and declaring it saves us. Becoming a servant or slave is part of our growth toward a more intimate walk with our Lord and essential to us in becoming a *huios*.

Remember, we begin our new life in the kingdom as *teknons*, but we are not to stay *teknons*. God's purpose is to see each of us grow up into a *huios*. To do that, we must submit to God's will and become a *doulos* (servant) like Jesus did.

Teknon, Doulos, Huios

Teknon is a Greek New Testament word denoting one who has been born. Emphasis is on the fact of the birth. A *teknon* has the seed of the Father. As mentioned previously, *doulos* denotes a slave or bondservant, one who has subjugated his will to another's. A *doulos* does the will of the Father. *Huios* denotes a mature son of God or the Son of God. Emphasis is on the depth of relationship and maturity. A *huios* has the nature of the Father.

We enter the kingdom of God as a newborn child, as a member of the family of God. We are accepted into that family not by our own merits but entirely on the merits of Jesus Christ who died for our sins and who redeemed us with a price—His own blood. As a newborn child or *teknon*, we desire earnestly the milk of the Word and seek to grow up in God. We learn that we must follow the example of Christ who subjugated His will entirely to the will of God, "Not My will but Yours be done" (Luke 22:42). We willingly become a *doulos* as we submit to the commands of God. We were once slaves of sin. Now we are slaves of righteousness; not to win justification, for it is done, but to develop into the *huios* of God. The whole of creation is waiting for the *huios* of God to be revealed, for they are copies of Jesus, the incarnate Word of God.

The new birth is more than a salvation experience. It is best understood as coming under new management. The control of sin is broken, and we come under the control or management of God. The central element in both the new birth and salvation is the understanding and declaration that Jesus is Lord. If He is Lord, then we are His servants. This salient component is often overlooked or missed. We tend to give the gospel a more positive spin emphasizing the love of God and the part about not going to hell.

But the truth remains and now stares you squarely in the face—if Jesus is Lord, then you must be, you might just as well admit it, a servant. The very nature of the relationship defines it. If God is Father, then you are His child. If God is Creator, then you are a creature. If God is Owner-Master-Lord, then you are slave-servant-steward.

You didn't have to obey all His commands to become born again, but now that you see and realize and have confessed that He is Lord, you must live like He is Lord. How do you do that? By obeying Him.

If you are truly prepared to have a relationship with God on the basis of that reality, then you are ready to become a *huios*. We are born again as children of God but we take the role of the servant as Jesus Himself modeled for us. We learn to do His will. We become a *huios* by first becoming a *doulos*. At first sight, the idea of being a slave is repellent. Our culture values freedom above all. What we neglect to consider is that the freedom our culture believes in is an illusion, because except by the grace of God, we are all slaves of sin.

Now we know what a *doulos* is—how do we become one?

Chapter Two

The Slave or
Servant Mentality

*Yet it shall not be so among you; but whoever desires to become great among you, let him be your servant. And whoever desires to be first among you, let him be your **slave**— just as the Son of Man did not come to be served, but to serve, and to give His life a ransom for many* (Matthew 20:26-28).

There are two slave mentalities; one is negative and one is positive. The negative slave mentality is also called the poverty mentality. An example from Scripture would be the children of Israel coming out of Egypt thinking themselves incapable of going into battle and wanting to go back to Egypt. This attitude is often seen today because of a limited concept of what God is able to provide. It is often a weird sort of revelation for Christians today for those with a poverty mentality to realize that Abraham, Isaac, Jacob, and Joseph were all multimillionaires. The covenant we have with God can bring prosperity—if we believe it, "that the blessing of Abraham might come upon the Gentiles..." (Gal. 3:14). The word *bless* literally means to empower to prosper.

You can't hold both the biblical concept of blessing and the poverty mentality simultaneously. To do so is double-minded. When the children of Israel were released as slaves from Egypt, they were instructed by God to take silver, gold, and clothing from the Egyptians. The Word testifies that they ransacked the Egyptians. They exited Egypt wealthy. Unfortunately, they also exited Egypt with an improper slave mentality. They did not know that their God could do *exceedingly and abundantly more than they could ask or **think*** (see Eph. 3:20).

The positive slave mentality can also be called the servant mentality. Believers have it who recognize God for who He really is. There are two vital revelations we need to embrace: who God is and who we are. God is our Father. We are children. God is the Creator. We are creatures. God is the Builder. We are the house. God is a general. We are His army. How we see God affects how we see ourselves. God is described in many ways, but the most important is the name of God—LORD. He is the Master. We are servants.

God is referred to as Father about 250 times in Scripture, which is a significant amount. He is referred to as God about 3,000 times, which is very significant. But He is referred to as Lord more than 7,000 times. Wow! That is His name. That is who He is. When you see Him as Father, you see yourself as a child of God; and when you see Him as Lord, then you have to see yourself as a bondservant or slave—*doulos*.

Good Company

Jesus was called a Servant of God in Acts 4:27. Moses was called the servant of God in Revelation 15:3. David, too, was called a servant of God in Acts 4:25. Each writer of the New Testament Books referred to himself as a servant of God. The New Testament writers saw themselves as servants and referred to themselves as servants— not sons. "Paul, *a bondservant of Jesus Christ,* called to be an apostle, separated to the gospel of God" (Rom. 1:1). This is not to deter us from seeing ourselves as God's sons. We are *teknon*. God is our Father. It is just to bring an emphasis that He is also our Lord and Master. And it is living as if He is our Lord and Master that will eventually get us to the point where we are the mature sons of God (*huios*). We must fully embrace this servant mentality.

We will be in good company if we accept that we are indeed servants or slaves of God. Being a slave does not seem very nice to us freedom lovers; but consider that back in the first century, the house slave of a wealthy Greek more than likely lived better than his free cousin back home on the farm. We may be slaves, but we are God's slaves and part of His household. That is vastly superior to the only other option—being a slave of sin.

There is a positive spin to being God's slave, but we must also face the reality of what this all means. It means we must willingly submit our will to God's will. It means obedience. The long and the short of it—we say we have a Lord, so we must live like we have a Lord. The only way to relate to our Lord is to be His servant. *If we confess with our mouths that Jesus is LORD,* not only do we become born again, but as newly born *teknons,* we come under new management—we become slaves of God.

> *What I am saying is that as long as an heir is underage* [a child], *he is no different from a slave, although he owns the whole estate* (Galatians 4:1 NIV).

We are both children and slaves of God. He is both our Father and our Master. We become a child of God quite easily by confessing that Jesus is Lord; but to become a mature son of God, we must also embrace the full import of this confession and adopt a slave or servant mentality. This is the road to becoming a *huios.*

> *But he who is greatest among you shall be your servant* (Matthew 23:11).

When I first started to see this concept of doing the will of God and the language of the New Testament which speaks of servants and slaves, I couldn't really relate to it. The truth was that I wanted to be great in the kingdom, but I wasn't too enamoured with the whole idea of being a servant, especially being *a servant of all.* I thought it might be nice to *have* a servant, but to be one? I had heard speakers discourse about leaders having the heart of a servant, but really, did they think we were buying what they were selling? I wasn't impressed by words, I wanted to see someone demonstrate this truth.

I had a rare experience years ago while attending a church in Calgary. This was many years before I was a pastor in Canmore. The pastor of the church in Calgary took some of us deacons with him to a leaders' conference at Mel Mullen's church in Red Deer. We were about to have a meal and were standing around visiting with other conference attendees. I was asked a number of times who I was and how many attended our church. When the inquirers learned that I was only a deacon—deacon also means servant, by the way—they quickly lost interest and moved on to someone more "connected."

There was one exception. I was chatting to a man in the buffet line who didn't seem to care about my status—he was genuine in his inquiries. I found out later he was the keynote speaker at the conference. He was from Portland, Oregon, and founded and led a church there called Bible Temple (now City Bible Church). Dick Iverson was his name. He seemed to me to be a true servant.

Recently in our house church, Huios House, where I am attempting to serve rather than just lead, we had a definitive experience. I was driving through town thinking about a sister in the Lord who had years earlier been part of our group but had been greatly disappointed by her Christian friend. I hadn't seen her for years. For some strange reason I thought about her and prayed for her. As I was coming to the end of the main street, I saw her waiting at the intersection. That's all there was to it at the time, but later the same week she showed up at Huios House, at our Saturday evening meeting. She was shy about showing up but was blessed that week, so she came again the following Saturday. She said, "Something is happening here. There is real love and respect here." The change she noticed was due to a new attitude of valuing every member and allowing them to speak. I think it has something to do with me being a servant.

Adopting a Servant Mentality

The first step in becoming a *doulos* is to know God by name. Moses was the one who first received the revelation of God's name as Lord. Moses was the greatest man in the whole Old Testament. He is called a servant of God. That is his highest accolade. Moses was not without faults, though. In fact, he was the ultimate sinner in that he is the only man who broke all of the Ten Commandments in one violent act (see Exod. 32:19). Paul called himself the greatest of all sinners (see 1 Tim. 1:15). Both Paul and Moses were educated men, highly used of God and prolific writers. They were first and foremost servants of God. So the first step is that we acknowledge that God is Lord.

Understanding what a lord is exactly, takes more time. We have no context in our culture to relate to the term lord or for that matter, the term servant. We understand from Scripture the idea of servant and Lord, but that is different from complete understanding and a working definition. To us, it is like a blueprint or two-dimensional drawing that looks confusing. An experienced architect looks at the blueprint and sees a three-dimensional mental picture. We see squiggles on a page. He sees the building. We need to see the building. Unfortunately, when it comes to seeing a lord or servant, there are very few role models currently available.

Truly understanding the dynamic of relating to a lord is something that will take time. I myself wrestle with it. In fact, at first, all you might see is your utter and complete failure at obedience. You come to realize how carnal you are—at least I did. While I hold strongly to the ideal of living under His lordship or government, I occasionally need to visit the fact that He is my Savior and High Priest. I take comfort in the fact that He won't give up on me, and He is aware of my weaknesses. If I confess my sins, He is faithful and just to forgive.

The idea of confessing sins is also difficult for some—it is for me. I find it hard to confess to something and ask for forgiveness knowing that I will repeat the offense again before the day or week is over. My pride tends to hinder my readiness to confess sins. I imagine that you don't have the pride that I do. I must confess that I have pride, and I don't always deal with it as I should. I once read somewhere that the amount of pride you have is inversely proportional to the amount you pray. Ouch! I am learning to overcome this by praying more in the Spirit. It really helps; I am glad that Jesus is my Savior. I hope this little diversion has been helpful, now back to lordship.

The first step is to acknowledge that Jesus is Lord. The next step is to discover what that means despite the obstacles that we face. God is aware that we fail to fully appreciate who He is. It's not a new problem. In Isaiah chapter 1, God actually vents His frustration. I think our fumbling attempts of at least trying to accept His rule please Him. We're on the right track.

> *Hear, O heavens, and give ear, O earth! For the Lord has spoken: I have nourished and brought up children, and they have **rebelled** against Me; the ox knows its **owner** and the donkey its **master's** crib; **But Israel does not know** [who I am]…. If you are willing and obedient, you shall eat the good of the land* (Isaiah 1:2-3,19).

Five Steps Toward Becoming a *Doulos*

We are handicapped by our Western culture to fully grasp what a lord is and how a servant behaves. We do, however, know the following:

1. We know that the concepts we need to *learn* are modeled in the Scriptures, so we can read them diligently. As we read, we can focus on the idea of gleaning as much as we can about servants and lords. Renewing our minds by consistent Bible reading is vital.

2. We know we must *do His will* not our own. "Thy kingdom come, Thy will be done" can be our daily *prayer*. God is our Master, but He is also our Helper. He will help us learn this important truth and make it real in our lives. I also find praying in the Spirit to be helpful.

3. We know we must *obey* His commands, "make disciples of all the nations…teaching them to obey everything that I've commanded you" (Matthew 28:19-20 NIV). So we can learn the commandments and ask God to help us obey them.

4. We can learn to grow in the *fear* of the Lord. Find out in Scripture what produces fear of the Lord. For example, tithing teaches us the fear of the Lord.

> *You shall truly tithe all the increase of your grain that the field produces year by year. And you shall eat before the LORD your God, in the place where He chooses to make His name abide, the tithe of your grain and your new wine and your oil, of the*

*firstborn of your herds and your flocks, that **you may learn to
fear the Lord** your God always* (Deuteronomy 14:22-23).

5. If we are committed to becoming a *doulos* and learning to
   be led of the Spirit, then we must face the fact that years of
   church attendance and church traditions have not as yet
   done the job. They may have helped a bit, but traditional
   church meetings are not designed to teach you to become
   Spirit-led. The true servant of God must hear and obey
   the Spirit. It's not something learned in a pew. So if we are
   serious about this, it would be valuable to relearn some
   things. We must drop the traditions of men that make the
   Word of God of no effect, because they will hinder us
   growing in this new direction. We must find like-minded
   believers who, like those in Malachi, "fear the Lord and
   speak to one another" to take the journey with us. We need
   their help and encouragement.

Often the unlearning of accepted traditions is more difficult than
learning new material. A person may not realize the depth to which
past evangelical teaching may hinder becoming a *huios*. I recom-
mend the books *Pagan Christianity* by Frank Viola and George
Barna, as well as, *The Messianic Church Arising* by Dr. Robert D. Heidler. They will help you see and make a break with some of our man-
made traditions that make the Word of no effect. In the chapters
ahead, we will explore the ramifications of evangelical theology and
compare and discuss kingdom theology as we turn hard soil into
prepared soil.

Chapter Three

The Heart of the Matter

When Jesus told the parable of the sower (see Matt. 13), He was speaking of the seed being the message of the kingdom. He spoke of the different types of soil: the hard soil of the paths, the shallow, gravely soil, the soil overgrown with weeds, and the good soil. When He gave the meaning of the parable, Jesus spoke of the wicked one stealing what was sown in the heart. The soil is the heart. There is, therefore, the hard-hearted, the faint-hearted, the half-hearted, and the full-hearted response to the kingdom message.

The good ground is where someone hears the word and understands it and bears fruit. The kingdom message is a message of the lordship of Jesus. It is a return to obedience to God and not simply a message about fire insurance. When you understand it, then you bear fruit of obedience like Jesus did. It starts with the heart. This is why we start with theology, so it can prepare the heart for understanding. What is the heart exactly?

The Heart Defined

*For as he **thinks** in his heart, so is he...* (Proverbs 23:7).

*...For out of the abundance of the heart the mouth **speaks*** (Matthew 12:34).

*A good man out of the good **treasure** of his heart brings forth good things, and an evil man out of the evil treasure brings forth evil things* (Matthew 12:35).

41

The heart is an organ of thought and the origin of things we speak. As a man thinks in his heart, so is he. Biblically, the word heart means inner core. It is not technical or scientific terminology. It means the part we cannot see or the part that is under the surface. The organ we associate with thought is the brain. The organ we call the heart is a blood pump. We confuse the Bible word heart with our blood pump. Sometimes the heart is seen as the seat of emotions or affections, and the brain is the locus of hard, cold logic. This is part of the confusion and not really biblically valid.

The heart of a man is a treasury like a thesaurus. It is perhaps best understood as the subconscious mind, and it resides in the brain. To say that something must go from the head to the heart while we gesture with our hands pointing from the head and then down to the blood pump is a very common misconception. The blood pump only pumps blood. It is a muscle. The brain is the seat of understanding both at a conscious and subconscious level. The writers of the Old Testament did not use modern psychological terms—they called it mind and heart. So when the Lord says He has written His laws in our hearts and minds, He means both in our subconscious and conscious.

The Subconscious

The subconscious is storehouse of all that you have seen, smelled, done, and heard your whole life. Things that are repeated over and over become patterns of thought. An architect once built a complex of office buildings with no connecting sidewalks. He had lawn planted, and after the summer, he instructed the sidewalk builders simply to install sidewalks where the lawns were worn down from foot traffic. The architect used the existing pathways and cemented them. Our minds are like that. There are pathways that become cemented into virtual freeways of thought.

Have you ever been driving your car thinking about something other than driving and find yourself automatically turning the way you most often go? Maybe you are going to work or your kids' school. For a split second you are confused until you realize that you have an appointment somewhere else. Your brain was on automatic—evidence of your subconscious doing the driving.

Once when I was on a short-term mission to the Philippines, we hired a car and driver to take us from Tabuk to a remote mountain village to visit and teach there. It was a long, hot trip up dusty logging roads. We were dropped of at the village's general store. The store had a Coca Cola fridge full of Coke. The thought of an ice cold Coke was refreshing to say the least. The store owner graciously offered us free Coke. Unfortunately, there was no electricity and the Coke was just as warm as we were.

We were hot and covered with dust, so the store owner graciously allowed us to shower in the outside shower in the back. Because we were in a remote area and all we could see was jungle, we said why not and proceeded to wash away the dust of the day. We took turns pouring buckets of water over each other in this little outside shower stall. Later we found out that the jungle was full of little houses we could not see. It seems our white, naked bodies had provided half the local population with entertainment that afternoon. No wonder everyone was smiling at us during the meeting that evening. I had thought at the time that they were just friendly.

After the evening meeting, we returned to the store to find that both the car and driver were gone. No explanation. The store owner graciously allowed us to rest inside the back area. I did not sleep though, because of all the visitors. I have never seen such big cockroaches! Finally at about 1 A.M. the driver showed up, so we headed back down the windy, logging roads to Tabuk. We all dozed off coming down the mountain—including the driver. We woke up in the mission compound in Tabuk at about 4 A.M.. When we realized the driver had been asleep for half the trip we postulated that the angels had got us safely down the mountain, but it may have simply been the driver's subconscious mind doing the driving. Where had our driver been all day and why was he late to take us home? It turns out that the store owner had used our driver and our gas for pick ups and deliveries for his business.

The subconscious can be the source for comments coming from your mouth. The heart of a man may be evil or good. "A good man out of the good treasure of his heart brings forth good things, and an evil man out of the evil treasure brings forth evil things" (Matt. 12:35). By the words of their mouths, you can tell what is in their hearts. Have you ever blurted something without thinking? *Where did that come from?* you wonder. Sometimes what you say is rude or inappropriate. Sometimes it is unrehearsed wit. Out of the abundance of the heart, the mouth speaks.

The subconscious is also a filter mechanism. You hear and process thousands of bits of information each day. You hear traffic sounds, buzzing, people talking, a radio, and baby cry, and your subconscious mind filters out what doesn't apply to you. A mother knows the cry of her own baby and when she hears a baby cry, her brain processes the sound of the cry and decides if it is her baby. If it is, she jumps up as quickly as a bullet leaves the muzzle of a gun. The man next to her filtered out the cry and is perhaps not even conscious of why the lady leaped up and ran into the next room.

The filtering function of the heart or subconscious also plays a major role in being Spirit-led. When the Spirit gives you a nudge or a holy hunch, your subconscious evaluates it and discerns its value. If your filter is programmed by your culture or the traditions of men, then the voice of the Spirit will be nonsense. If your filter is programmed by the Word of God, then the Spirit will be allowed to be expressed.

Programming the Subconscious

There are two ways to program the subconscious. Traumatic experiences can greatly imprint the subconscious mind. The initial infilling of the Holy Spirit is an example. Being shot is as well. Not all traumatic experiences are as pleasant as being baptized in the Holy Spirit. The more common method of programming is repetition. That is how the traditions of men have been firmly planted.

The subconscious is quite powerful. As a filter, it acts as a judge deciding what is important what is not, what makes sense and what does not, what to believe and what to reject. If you are raised in a ghetto, you may have been taught all your life to hate "the oppressors" who you believe forced you to live in squalor. If later in life you meet an "oppressor," you will have difficulty seeing any good in that person. Your programmed response will be one of hatred and distrust.

My father fought the Nazis in World War II, and he hated all Germans, which is understandable. I, however, did not see fellow soldiers killed by Germans, and I have a different feeling toward Germans. I like Germans—except when they are aggressive in the ski lift line. I prefer the British in that regard. They queue up rather politely.

The subconscious is a filter when it comes to our theology. When I wrote *Understanding the Kingdom of God* (part of which is included in this book as Part II Kingdom Foundations), I had a friend proofread it and give me comments. He was at odds with something I said about water baptism and set out to prove to me that baptism does not save people only the blood can save people. He had the normal evangelical programming that the only doctrine of consequence is justification.

So when he saw the word saved in the context of water baptism, he freaked. There was once a practice of waiting until your deathbed to be baptized based on the idea that it was baptism that removed your sins. So perhaps he was concerned that I had been captivated by a heresy. Anyway, long story short, I pointed to First Peter 3:21 and his eyes opened wide. He said, "Wow. I've never seen that before."

> There is also an antitype which now saves us—baptism (not the removal of the filth of the flesh, but the answer of a good conscience toward God), through the resurrection of Jesus Christ (1 Peter 3:21).

Just so you don't freak out as well, let me be understood. Jesus which is Greek for Joshua, or Yeshua, means "Yahweh saves" or Savior. In a real way, everything Jesus does for us, saves us. Saves us from what, is the question:

- The shed blood saves us from sins.

- The water of baptism saves us from the power of sin to bring us back under its control.

- The baptism of the Holy Spirit saves us from trying to do the impossible—live the Christian life in our own strength.

- The truth saves us from error.

- Water saves us from thirst.

- Food saves us from hunger.

- Healing saves us from sickness.

- Deliverance saves us from evil spirits.

- Wealth saves us from poverty.

- A spouse saves us from "burning" (see 1 Cor. 7:9).

Everything God gives us saves us from something. "Saved" is a bigger and broader subject than mere justification.

Just out of curiosity, did you freak a little bit when I brought up the idea that baptism saves us? Did your subconscious scream, "Red alert! Danger!" That is an example of your evangelical programming. When I first heard the idea of spiritual mapping, I rejected it because I knew the words spiritual mapping do not appear anywhere in Scripture. I also rejected it because I saw intercessors doing spiritual mapping in a way that did not sit well with me. It troubled my mind. Later I read some books on it and realized what the authors were really trying to do, and I was OK with it. But I wasn't OK with what the intercessors I knew were doing because they hadn't really understood the concept at that time. Sometimes the filter works to your advantage, but sometimes it works to your disadvantage. It depends on what has been programmed into your mind.

Joshua was told to program his subconscious with the law of Moses. He was promised that if he meditated on the Word day and night, he would prosper.

> *This Book of the Law shall not depart from your mouth, but you shall meditate in it day and night, that you may observe to do according to all that is written in it. For then you will make your way prosperous, and then you will have good success (Joshua 1:8).*

Meditate in this instance means to say it over and over. Repetition equals programming the subconscious. This is why the healing evangelists are always promoting that you buy their cassette tapes and listen to them over and over. They have a valid point. Often the only way to undo programming of years of unbelief is to have new programming repeated to the extend it overwrites the old.

The Roman Centurion

The Roman centurion presents an intriguing example of subconscious programming. He was so used to servants and soldiers obeying his commands that his mind understood at a subconscious level that Jesus also had an authority to be obeyed.

> *Now when Jesus had entered Capernaum, a centurion came to Him, pleading with Him, saying, "Lord, my servant is lying at home paralyzed, dreadfully tormented." And Jesus said to him, "I will come and heal him." The centurion answered and said, "Lord, I am not worthy that You should come under my roof. But only speak a word, and my servant will be healed. For I also am a man under authority, having soldiers under me. And I say to this one, 'Go,' and he goes; and to another, 'Come,' and he comes; and to my servant, 'Do this,' and he does it." When Jesus heard it, He marveled, and said to those who followed, "Assuredly, I say to you, I have not found such great faith, not even in Israel! And I say to you that many will come from east and west, and sit down with Abraham, Isaac, and Jacob in the kingdom of heaven. But the sons of the kingdom will be cast out into outer darkness. There will be weeping and gnashing of teeth." Then Jesus said to the centurion, "Go your way; and as you have believed, so let it be done for you." And his servant was healed that same hour* (Matthew 8:5-13).

Jesus marveled at the centurion's faith. The centurion had *subconscious faith*. It is one thing to have a conscious faith, but if the subconscious doesn't buy it, the conscious is overruled. We can confuse "hoping and wishing and praying and hoping" with real heartfelt faith. The heart is the subconscious. Faith in the heart is subconscious faith—faith like the centurion's. The centurion came by this faith honestly. It grew through the many times the same experience was repeated, "'Do this,' and he does it."

We have subconscious faith that our chair will hold our weight. We have sat in that same chair, or one like it, countless times, so now we don't even think about it being strong enough. We just sit. That is until the day when the chair collapses beneath us and our subconscious is reprogrammed by a traumatic experience.

This is why we can go forward in a healing meeting and receive prayer but not get healed. We acknowledge God has the power to heal. We know that others have been healed. We go forward wishing to get healed, but we don't have subconscious heart faith. We must have heart faith, we must believe in our hearts according to Romans 10:9.

We are at a distinct disadvantage. Jesus demonstrated His ability to heal before His disciples over and over and over again. They were programmed to expect healing just like we expect a chair to hold us. Peter became so accustomed to healing that not only was his subconscious totally convinced, it oozed out into his shadow, and his shadow healed people. The people were also so used to witnessing healing that they had subconscious faith as well. I want that kind of faith.

*And believers were increasingly added to the Lord, multitudes of both men and women, so that they brought the sick out into the streets and laid them on beds and couches, that at least the **shadow** of Peter passing by might fall on some of them. Also a multitude gathered from the surrounding cities to Jerusalem, bringing sick people and those who were tormented by unclean spirits, and **they were all healed** (Act 5:14-16).*

Imprinting

The absolute best way to become a *huios* is to be discipled by a *huios*. Peter was discipled by the *Huios*. We are at a distinct disadvantage in that regard. Unfortunately we do not have many *huios* role models available to teach us. There have been some who have fought the fight of faith and won a way to victory. I am thinking of Kenneth Hagin who developed subconscious faith for healing on his own with no encouragement from others. John Wimber is another fine example of a man with subconscious faith for healing, but his testimony tells of an intense struggle for years before victory was in hand. Saint, do not give up in your fight to become a son of God, a *huios*. Saturate your heart with the Gospels until the *huios* way of life is imprinted. Yes, the path before you is difficult because you have no one to disciple you. You do, however, have the Spirit of God. There is a way.

Home Is Where the Heart Is

The heart of the matter is that the heart is an organ of thought and source of speech. The heart can be programmed by repetition to have a deep and enduring faith. The heart is best described as the subconscious mind and should not to be equated to the blood pump. It is unlikely you will undo years of thinking of your heart as being in your chest in one reading of this book—unless it was very traumatic for you. But please begin to cast off the old thinking patterns and embrace a new and better understanding of heart so that you can make application to program it appropriately.

So the heart and mind reside in the brain. What resides in the chest? Maybe just organs. The Hebrews believed that the spirit resided in the belly or gut. We sometimes attest to a gut feeling. Jesus said out of your *belly* rivers of water shall flow, "He that believeth on Me, as the scripture hath said, out of his belly shall flow rivers of living water. (But this spake He of the Spirit, which they that believe on him should receive…)" (John 7:38-39 KJV). The Holy Spirit flows from the belly, so perhaps the spirit lives in the gut.

Many still think of the heart being synonymous with the spirit. They haven't heard the reasons to consider it to be the subconscious mind. Armed with what is perhaps a more accurate understanding of heart, you can read the words of Scripture and take new meaning from their words.

Knowing that we can program the subconscious by repetition and that the subconscious acts like a filter, what should we do?

*And do not be conformed to this world, but be **transformed by the renewing of your mind**, that you may prove what is that good and acceptable and perfect will of God (Romans 12:2).*

Repetitive, consistent input of the law or teachings of the Word, as with Joshua, will renew your mind, which will reprogram your heart. Your heart is a filter. You need a clean filter, especially if you are to become Spirit-led. If the Spirit prompts you to do something, your heart will filter it. It is absolutely essential that your filter knows the Word so that the prompting of the Spirit can be yielded to and the prompting of the flesh can be recognized as such and rejected. Daily, consistent Bible reading helps you become a *huios*.

Where Is Your Treasure?

Since from the heart comes the issues of life, it is the heart we must reprogram with the truth. We do that with new understanding and wisdom, and we do that with new practices that repeatedly reinforce it. One of the ways of tracing the intent of the heart is to see where we give or spend our money. "For where your treasure is, there your heart will be also" (Matt. 6:21). What we do with money not only can give insight to the heart, but it is also part and parcel of being a servant of the Lord.

Chapter Four

Heart Barometer

What we do with our money indicates where our heart is. In some ways, it serves as a barometer or a measuring device on reality. Tithing is a subject that is controversial, but deserves some consideration in light of what the Lord Jesus said in Matthew 5:

> *For assuredly, I say to you, till heaven and earth pass away, one jot or one tittle will by no means pass from the law till all is fulfilled. Whoever therefore **breaks one of the least of these commandments,** and teaches men so, shall be called least in the kingdom of heaven; but whoever does and teaches them, he shall be called great in the kingdom of heaven* (Matthew 5:18-19).

Tithing has been called both a blessing and a burden. I have studied this topic extensively and written articles about it. I would like to share a few insights that may surprise you. I offer three insights about tithing from a framework of living in the kingdom of God and as tools in becoming a *huios*.

Insight One

The first insight is that Malachi chapter 3 is in the New Testament—not structurally, but in intent. If you read Malachi chapter 3, you will note that it speaks about Elijah whom Jesus tells us in the Gospels is John the Baptist. God is speaking from a future perspective. Note that tithing is a way of returning to God, and that failure to pay the tithe was seen by Him as robbing Him personally. When we fail to tithe, we are not robbing the church or the temple or the Levites, we are robbing God. Let's look at it closely.

> *"Behold, I send **My messenger, and he will prepare the way before Me**. And the Lord, whom you seek, will suddenly come to His temple, even the Messenger of the covenant, in whom you delight. Behold, He is coming," says the Lord of hosts* (Malachi 3:1).

> *Remember the Law of Moses, My servant, which I commanded him in Horeb for all Israel, with the statutes and judgments. Behold, I will send you **Elijah the prophet** before the coming of the great and dreadful day of the Lord* (Malachi 4:4-5).

We have the reference to John the Baptist. Jesus declares it in Matthew 11:14. Next we see God makes an interesting claim. His people can return to Him by tithing.

> *"For I am the Lord, I do not change; therefore you are not consumed, O sons of Jacob. Yet from the days of your fathers, you have gone away from My ordinances and have not kept them. **Return to Me, and I will return to you**," says the Lord of hosts. "But you said, '**In what way shall we return?**' Will a man rob God? Yet you have robbed Me! But you say, 'In what way have we robbed You?' In tithes and offerings. You are cursed with a curse, for you have robbed Me, even this whole nation. Bring all the tithes into the storehouse, that there may be food in My house, and try Me now in this," says the Lord of hosts, "If I will not **open for you the windows of heaven** and **pour out for you such blessing** that there will not be room enough to receive it. And I will **rebuke the devourer** for your sakes, so that he will not destroy the fruit of your ground, nor shall the vine fail to bear fruit for you in the field," says the Lord of hosts; "And **all nations will call you blessed**, for you will be a delightful land," says the Lord of hosts* (Malachi 3:6-12).

If you really look at the Book of Malachi, you will agree that it is very New Testament. God is looking to the day when Jesus will come. Why, in light of His thinking about the coming of the Lord Jesus, does God say that the path back to Him is to pay tithes? Tithing is not a step of entering the kingdom, nor is it a required step in salvation. The essence of the message of the kingdom is the lordship of Jesus. We must simply confess that He is Lord.

Why does God mention tithes?

Tithing was done before the law, was taught in the law, and was briefly referenced by the Lord when He rebuked the Pharisees who tithed on their herb gardens. He told them that they had missed some important things but to keep on tithing. Tithing is highlighted in the Book of Malachi, which was the last word God gave for four or five centuries. But what has tithing to do with returning to the Lord? Think about it.

The Lord is the Lord of all the earth, or the land. In Genesis 1:1, the word earth is the Hebrew word for land. He owns it. We live here, but God owns here. He is Lord of the land, our landlord. We prove our faith in the Lord of the land by acts of faith—faith without deeds is dead (see James 2:17)—that demonstrate that we really believe that He is indeed Lord. We pay Him rent. This is what the tithe is—a very reasonable rent. As rent, the tithe does not earn us a place in God's family but shows that we truly respect the place that He holds as Lord.

For truly acknowledging His right to rule us, God promises an abundance of things that we all want and need. An open heaven means answered prayer. Blessing means empowerment to prosper. Rebuke the devourer means protection and deliverance from evil. These are things that we want, yes?

It is good to confess that Jesus is Lord, but now you must live like it. Show others that you put God before money. Show others that He is Lord of all your life.

Insight Two

The second insight into tithing comes from the Law of Moses. In Deuteronomy 14, Moses first makes mention of tithing. People need to read this because this is not at all what many think tithing means. This passage is surprising.

*You shall truly tithe all the increase of your grain that the field produces year by year. And **you shall eat** before the Lord your God, **in the place** where **He chooses** to make His name abide, the tithe of your grain and your new wine and your oil, of the firstborn of your herds and your flocks, **that you may learn to fear the Lord** your God always. But if the journey is too long for you, so that you are not able to carry the tithe, or if the place where the Lord your God chooses to put His name is too far from you, when the Lord your God has blessed you, then you shall exchange it for money, take the money in your hand, and go to the place which the Lord your God chooses. And you shall spend that money **for whatever your heart desires:** for oxen or sheep, for wine or similar drink, **for whatever your heart desires;** you shall eat there before the Lord your God, **and you shall rejoice,** you and your household. You shall not forsake the Levite who is within your gates, for he has no part nor inheritance with you* (Deuteronomy 14:22-27).

Tithing teaches the fear of the Lord. This is something the church needs. Some teach against tithing, but why remove a practice that teaches us something as important as the fear of the Lord?

The place where you bring the tithe is in the place He chooses, not simply the temple. This is an eternal truth. The fact that the temple is destroyed does not destroy the tithe, because we have prima facie evidence right here in Deuteronomy 14 that the tithe goes to where God chooses. He is not locked into the temple. The tithe belongs to Him, not the temple.

Did you notice, and I bet you didn't, that you get to spend the tithe on a feast? Does that blow your religious mind? You get to eat! Maybe you should go back and read the passage again. And you get to buy whatever your heart desires. Now, remember, it was once a year at harvest, so don't justify spending your tithe on the weekly groceries. A portion of the tithe was consumed, the rest donated. Did you also see that rejoicing is part of tithing? Imagine that! Tithing is a joy, not a burden. Now we will look at a second mention of tithing by Moses.

Insight Three

*When you have finished laying aside all the tithe of your increase in the third year—the year of tithing—and have given it to the Levite, the stranger, the fatherless, and the widow, so that they may eat within your gates and be filled, then **you shall say** before the Lord your God: "**I have removed the holy tithe from my house,** and also have given them to the Levite, the stranger, the fatherless, and the widow, **according to all Your commandments** which You have commanded me; I have not transgressed Your commandments, nor have I forgotten them. I have not eaten any of it when in mourning, nor have I removed any of it for an unclean use, nor given any of it for the dead. **I have obeyed the voice of the Lord my God, and have done according to all that You have commanded me.** Look down from Your holy habitation, from heaven, and **bless Your people Israel** and the land which You have given us, just as You swore to our fathers, 'a land flowing with milk and honey'"* (Deuteronomy 26:12-15).

What really speaks to me in this passage is the personal nature of tithing. This was not an impersonal tax but rather an involved, deep discussion with the Lord Himself. You can clearly see the elements of **stewardship** as the tither goes over the "books" with his master. "I have obeyed and done what you commanded," sounds like the fear of the Lord to me. It sounds like someone who sees himself as a servant honoring the Lord personally. Notice, as well, the expectation of the tithing servant as he expresses the hope springing from the obedience of faith that he will, in fact, be rewarded. Faith expects rewards. Maybe we have been tithing regularly or faithfully, but have we been tithing in faith expecting a reward? Do we take full advantage of this very personal aspect of tithing?

The three insights into tithing include the idea that tithing was a way to return to the Lord as it is a way of honoring the Lord of all the earth. This is not a salvation issue but a stewardship issue. Tithing teaches the fear of the Lord. Robbing God teaches us not to fear the Lord. A second insight is the fact that God chooses the place where you tithe, and the tithe contains a component of feasting and rejoicing. Third, tithing is very personal between you and your Lord and is very much a faith exercise that looks forward to the rewards mentioned in Malachi.

Application

Now we make an application with regard to tithing. In light of what you have just read and in light of our goal to become Spirit-led, why not turn tithing into an exercise where you can practice hearing from God. Each month or each pay period, speak to the Lord and tell Him you are paying Him the tithe. Act like a steward giving his report to his Master. Then ask Him where to direct it. One month the Lord told me to give the tithe ($600) to a Christian outreach, to the poor; and give an additional $500 to a mission in Africa. More recently, I was directed to give $500 to a daughter of one of our members who is serving as a missionary in the Dominican Republic; and my wife was told to give $1,000 to the girl's sister who was getting married and who is ready to go to the mission field. Sometimes we don't hear anything, so we wait a bit and then by default direct it to our local church. The fun part is learning to hear and obey the Lord. We also expect to receive bountifully from the Lord—pressed down, shaken together, and running over (see Luke 6:38).

Discerning the Difference

Tithing in today's traditional church setting at times appears to be little more than a legalistic method of fundraising for clergy and building projects. I say traditional church because even the most Pentecostal Protestant church still carries baggage from Roman times. The way we structure our meetings, the way we conduct church, dictates how we interpret and apply Scriptures. We see the local church building as the temple. We are taught to bring the tithe faithfully into the temple. We have given out of a desire to obey Scripture, but in a way determined by our church traditions. Despite our good intentions, the tithe has sometimes been misused, and we have sometimes been manipulated by strong appeals.

Paying a tenth of our income seems rigid in our "God is all mercy and forgiveness" milieu. Antinomianism abounds in the liberty we enjoy. Tithing seems at odds with that liberty. We have been influenced by both legalism and lawlessness. The original intention of God for the tithe has been sidetracked. Most of us who tithe do it with a limited understanding and fail to realize its full benefits.

The *practice* of tithing in today's church may be legalistic, but the *concept* of tithing is not. Tithing was not part of the law of offerings and sacrifices for removing sin. Therefore it was not done away with by the sacrifice of Jesus. Tithing was practiced before Moses' time. And as we just studied, it appears in the teachings of Moses. Moses teaches that tithing helps us learn a fear of the Lord and is accompanied by feasting, rejoicing, and personal conversation with the Lord Himself. It is a covenant-stewardship issue. He explains it will lead to blessings and prosperity (not justification or removal of sin).

Jesus tells us He did not do away with the commands of the law, and He expects us to do and to teach even the least of them. Jesus did not teach us to abandon tithing or to adjust our thinking in this regard, as He did with food laws. Historically, tithing was at least partially reinstated each time Israel had a revival. It seemed to be a recurring theme.

Finally, as God is thinking about invading earth with His ultimate plan to redeem humankind, the kingdom of God, His thoughts turn in Malachi to tithing. He is offended that humankind has rejected His right to rule as Lord of all the earth evidenced in our refusal to pay rent. He declares that we have robbed Him personally—not that we have robbed the temple or the Levites or the poor. He desires to have His people return to Him. He is willing and waiting to bless us.

Returning to Him

How do we return to Him? By tithes and offerings. Why them? Because intrinsic to the whole relationship between man and his Creator is the respect man must give his Sovereign. Tithing teaches us the fear of the Lord. *Tithing is the visible manifestation of the respect we owe God.* Tithing shows that *we get it!* We are His creation. We are stewards. We are destined to rule and reign—under His management.

*Then those who feared the Lord spoke to one another, and the Lord listened and heard them; so a book of remembrance was written before Him for **those who fear the Lord** and who meditate on His name. **"They shall be Mine,"** says the Lord of hosts, "On the day that I make them My jewels. And I will spare them as a man spares **his own son who serves him."** Then you shall again discern between **the righteous and the wicked,** between one who serves God and one who does not serve Him* (Malachi 3:16-18).

Tithing helps us learn to fear the Lord, and God listens to those who fear Him. "They shall be mine," says the Lord. This is not a religious practice God wants us to perform but something personal. This is part of covenant. Like the marriage covenant, it is a personal relationship. Do you want God to listen to your prayers? Do you want to return to God in a full understanding of covenant relationship? Do you want wisdom? Do you want to be blessed?

Tithing is intended to be a blessing. It is intended to be personal. It is supposed to provide a joyous feast. The feast has aspects of remembering the goodness of God and giving God praise. Tithing has an aspect of speaking to the Lord as a steward giving an account of himself. Upon having the Lord check His "books," the steward could ask for his rewards.

Being in Christ does not remove us from this position of being a servant of God. It is only in Christ that we can be true servants. Only as a servant do we fully relate to our Lord. We are children who serve our Father. If being in Christ means we are stewards, then being in Christ means we show respect, or fear, toward the Lord our God with the tithe.

Being in Christ means that we have capacity for greater communication with our Lord with greater rejoicing and greater capacity for His blessing. In means we can learn by the Spirit to tithe according to the Word. We shouldn't be bound by religious tradition to give where tradition tells us. We can give in faith to God personally to where the Spirit directs, and we can expect rewards. We can give in joy. We can become hilarious givers. We can be blessed servants as God intended. We can be on the road to becoming a *huios*.

Tithing as God Directs

The steward prospers with the Master. In God's economy, when you make Him the boss, you will prosper as He does. I mentioned that paying a tithe is a stewardship issue that shows that we really do get the fact that He is Lord. Often when praying for someone to be healed we ask them to do something that they couldn't before to show that they are being healed. Tithing is something we do to show that our understanding of who Jesus is, has been healed. Tithing teaches us the fear of the Lord, which is the beginning of wisdom (see Ps. 111:10). Proper tithing has as one of its many benefits the development of wisdom.

Tithing in faith rather than just tithing faithfully—regularly, automatically—has the added benefit of rewards. Faith is rewarded. Tithing in faith should help us grow our faith. Faith comes by hearing. The concept introduced previously was to tithe to God directly. You pay Him the tithe and then ask Him to direct where it should go. This is a good exercise in learning to hear and obey God. Learning to hear and obey the Spirit is, of course, part of becoming Spirit-led, becoming *huios*. You ask God to direct your tithing and your giving. This can produce wonderful results.

Once you have recovered from the shock of realizing that you are allowed to pray about where to direct your tithe, all kinds of possibilities open. If for years you have been tithing to your local church, you may feel like you are robbing needed income from the local church. There are a couple of things you need to know. It is possible that much of the tithe will be directed by God to your local church. I typically give 75 percent or more to my local church. I direct some of my tithing and giving through the local church to ministries, missionaries, and even the poor. It all depends on what your local church is doing.

There are months when I don't really get a clear idea from the Lord where to direct my tithe. I pray to Him and give Him the tithe, but nothing jumps to mind as to where to direct it. At those times, I may just direct the tithe money to something on my heart, usually things in which our local church is involved. The point is to keep practicing, asking God to direct in the hope that you will hear Him more clearly.

The traditions of men have been so well-ingrained into your heart, subconscious, that it is hard to break out of the mold, so it is good to have some guidelines from the Word of God. Since the Spirit agrees with the Word in this way, you will be better grounded. You will have more success and less chance of going wonky—going off track.

What does the Word say about directing our tithes?

First of all, we are allowed to spend part of the tithe on a feast. Does that mean your tithe can go to the monthly grocery bill? Not likely! The people of Israel did the tithe once or twice a year (at harvest time). So it is not about a daily feasting but an occasional event. In our church, we suggest that members, if so led, can direct some of the tithe toward the cost of our monthly love feast. All you need are twelve families to tithe once per year and all twelve months are covered. This application is not used much though, at least not yet.

Another area of feasting is the kind were we feed on the Word. The tithe can go to the storehouse so that there is meat in the house of the Lord. That originally referred to the physical feeding of the workers at the Lord's house, but it could also be applied to feeding ourselves spiritually. We encourage people to be free to direct money toward the costs of conferences, DVDs, and books that will enrich them spiritually. We also help each other pay for these things as well.

The early church gave money collected to traveling teachers, including apostles and prophets, who were church planting and to the poor. That means it is always legitimate to direct funds, as the Lord leads, to teachers, missionaries, and the poor. I often give to a mission in Africa that provides for Christian workers as well as giving to the poor. Sometimes we will be led to send to an organization that feeds the poor or provides for orphans. Sometimes we will even send to a television evangelist like Sid Roth, host of *It's Supernatural.* I try to wherever possible hear from God as to whom to send His money, but I am also guided by the mission statement of the people I could be supporting.

Practical guidelines include the following. Do they have a mission statement that includes preaching the kingdom, healing the sick, and making disciples? If not, I am guided by Jesus' statement, "Let the dead bury their own dead" (Matt. 8:22). Sorry if that offends, but there are so many demands put on us every month to give to this and that. We need some guidelines. We need to know when to say no. Another guideline is, "Do I know them personally?" I always prefer to support those who were sent out from where I live or people I know personally. Failing that, they are at least known to be of high integrity. Do they just provide food for the poor or do they also lead people to Christ? I want to be confident that money I give is invested in growing the kingdom of God. We typically support the person, not the mission; and we also contribute to the needs of retired missionaries.

So biblically speaking, the tithe can go to provide a feast, provide for the poor, and provide for Christian workers—apostles, missionaries, elders, deacons, etc. It should be given first to God personally, and then as a steward, you should listen to hear where God wants to direct it each month. When you make tithing personal, it can become fun. You talk to God. You listen to God. You obey God. You grow up in God. Sometimes you are blessed when you direct the Lord's money to a need and the feedback you get is how it perfectly met a specific need for that person or that mission. Not only does the recipient feel great and know that God really does care for them, but you are blessed as well to have been part of a miracle. The serendipity is that what used to be an automatic ritual now becomes a method for becoming a *huios*. This of course extends to giving as well.

Giving and Expecting

Giving is what you contribute in addition to the tithe, and the scope is much broader. When you give, expect God to give back to you in abundance. The first tenth belongs to God, but once it is tithed, the rest of your money is blessed. In my experience, giving yields even greater fruit than tithing. Years ago, before I retired from pastoring, we invited Phil Vogel from Guildford, England, to visit our church. Phil was so willing to come to Canmore to teach us, that he said don't worry about paying his way.

He shared for a week, and the church was blessed, so I took up a love offering. It only came to $350 dollars, more or less. I rounded it up a wee bit with funds in our general account to $400. I knew his airfare was $1,100, and I felt that $400 was not enough. I am not allowed to juggle the books, but I was allowed to direct part of my salary to Phil. I gave half my salary that month, specifically $1,000 after tithe dollars to make the love offering $1400. This was more in keeping with the needs Phil had, and since he had labored among us and blessed us, I felt he deserved to be blessed.

I knew God would take care of my family, even if we had to eat potatoes and porridge for the rest of the month. God did! The very next week I received cheque in the mail for $10,000. The sender was not in our congregation and did not know my needs. The person was simply allowing God to direct the giving. The note said, "Here is some money God told me to send you for the kingdom of God." Giving really is fun, especially when you get a big cheque!

I encourage you to use tithing and giving as part of your method to practice hearing and obeying the Spirit. It really works; and if you miss hearing God a couple of times, don't despair—keep trying. Giving as God directs means you are partnering with God. You get useful feedback. You give in faith, and therefore can and should expect God to richly provide for you. Jesus said, "Give, and it will be given to you: good measure, pressed down, shaken together, and running over will be put into your bosom" (Luke 6:38). We don't give like we're buying a lottery ticket. We give in obedience, and our faith has an expectation that God tells the truth.

I encourage you to:

- Give generously.

- Give in faith.

- Give as you hear from God as He directs you.

- Use these opportunities to practice hearing the Spirit.

You will grow as a *huios*.

You will be blessed.

Chapter Five

Perspective

I have already mentioned that one of the challenges we have in becoming a *huios* is our lack of actual role models. Having a *huios* available to disciple us would make things a bit easier. Another challenge is the fact that the concept of being God's servant is pretty much unknown and unsavory to us. We normally don't think that way. If the kingdom perspective that Jesus is first and foremost Lord is correct, then we must adjust our perspective of how we see ourselves. We must adapt our thinking to coincide with God's perspective of who we are. We are servants. Again, there are very few master-servant relationships that are role models for us to observe. We are really unprepared to put this concept into action.

We are programmed to think in terms of what the Savior can do for us rather than how we serve the Lord. Our theology is church-centered not kingdom-centered. I have heard evangelistic appeals that make it sound like Jesus is so focussed on your individual needs that you would be doing Him a personal favor if you were to ask Him into your heart.

I have heard a message from the pulpit telling us that the church is the most important thing of all to God. The preacher continued to say that because the church is God's highest priority, the church should be our highest priority as well. Husband, how would you like it if you were told the greatest love of your life should be your wife and the greatest love of her life should be herself? Not likely. Our highest priority should be the Lord.

Our appeals that make God seem desperate and sinners seem important has tainted our theology. Our sermons emphasizing how important we are as individuals and how Jesus is wanting, waiting, and willing to meet our every need has affected our thinking. Our replacing a proper confession that Jesus is Lord with a prayer asking the Savior into our hearts has weakened our understanding and produced newborns that are sickly. The fact that meetings cater to us as audiences has reinforced our self-importance. We have become self-centered not God-centered in our theology and practice.

Despite the fact that babies are cute and wonderful, they are also the most demanding and selfish, self-centered people. They squawk, and we run to meet their needs. They are catered to night and day. The only thing that may actually be more ironic is that we have to walk behind our dogs and pick up their poop. With babies we have to feed them, pass them toys, pick up the toys, and pass them again, clean their diapers, etc. One of the things a baby learns during his or her first few years is: "I rule." Self is firmly on the throne.

The same thing is prevalent in the church. We are still, for the most part, babies. We are self-centered spiritually. I am not saying that all Christians are selfish, immature people. Many Christians I know are wonderful, sweet, and selfless. I am not saying that we are in general self-centered; I am saying in relation to how we interact with God, we are still babies. We still believe that we are able to live like spoiled brats who throw their porridge on the floor.

Baby-like Christians hope God in His infinite mercy will overlook transgressions. After all, we are under grace. Grace unfortunately is used as an excuse for failure and lawlessness. God is indeed merciful, but as babies we take it to an extreme that ignores the fact that He is also just—and He also Lord. Grace has been misunderstood.

What is grace supposed to be? How would you define it? How does the Lord define it?

The Wonderful World of Grace

I define grace as divine enablement or divine power. How does church-centered evangelical theology define grace? Chances are they have a vague collage of ideas involving "unmerited" and "mercy" rather than a concise definition.

"For you are not under law but under grace" (Rom. 6:14). Grace is contrasted with law and law means rules to follow. That must mean there are no rules involved with grace. When you can't pay a debt on time, they might extend you a grace period, which means they cut you some slack. So grace means a lessening or slackening of God's commands, "…not according to our works, but according to His own purpose and grace…" (2 Tim. 1:9). Grace means God does it all, and no effort on our part is required.

The word gracious means kind, benevolent, courteous, merciful, and compassionate. Exodus 34:6 says God is gracious. Grace and gracious seem like similar words so we equate their meanings. Grace, therefore, means merciful and compassionate. Many Christians equate grace with mercy. Note: Although grace and gracious relate in English, in the Greek they are two different words. Grace is *charis*, and gracious is *chrestos*. So it is inaccurate to equate grace and gracious.

Grace is defined as unmerited favor, but because we are unclear about what favor is, we emphasize that it's unmerited. The emphasis on *unmerited,* or undeserved, makes grace seem more like mercy than anything else. The evangelical collage of grace leads us to picture it as no rules to follow, no effort required, the bar has been lowered, and it pretty much equates to mercy.

If grace is *unmerited favor,* then what is favor? After all favor is the noun and unmerited is just the adjective. The noun is more important. Favor is derived from the Greek word *charis. Charis* is translated as joy or grace. *Charis* means favor, joy, or grace.

Luke chapter 1 tells the story of Mary's dialogue with Gabriel. Mary is told that she is highly favored and will conceive a son. She brings up the small detail of her virginity, and Gabriel explains that the Holy Spirit and His power will accomplish it. This is perhaps one of the best explanations of grace. *Grace is the empowering presence of the Spirit. Grace means divine energy or power or divine influence.*

That is why we are told we are not saved by works—human effort, human work, human power—we are saved by grace—divine effort, divine work, divine power. It requires energy to convert us from dead to living. That is why Jesus was full of grace. He was full of divine power. He healed the sick. He raised the dead. He did these things with the energy of the Spirit. It says of Jesus that He had the Spirit without measure. That's a lot of grace.

Charis also means joy. The joy of the Lord is our strength, power. In the presence of the Lord is fullness of joy—grace, strength, power. The presence of the Lord is with us and in us. Christ in us is the hope of glory. I speak of the Holy Spirit. The Holy Spirit is grace to us.

The Holy Spirit = Grace

What is the essential difference between the old and new covenant? Hebrews 8 and Jeremiah 31:31 tells us that the law is written in our hearts and minds. It is the same law as the Old Testament. The difference in the New Covenant is that we are given the Spirit, or grace or divine power, to actually *do* God's commands.

> *I will give you a new heart and put a new spirit within you; I will take the heart of stone out of your flesh and give you a heart of flesh. I will put **My Spirit** within you and **cause you to walk in** My statutes, and **you will keep** My judgments and **do them** (Ezekiel 36:26-27).*

Please read the following excerpts and consider that grace, the Holy Spirit or divine energy, has been given to us to enable us to work:

> *As each one has received a gift, minister it to one another, as good stewards of the manifold grace of God (1 Peter 4:10).*

> *For I am the least of the apostles, who am not worthy to be called an apostle, because I persecuted the church of God. But by the grace of God I am what I am, and His **grace** toward me was not in vain; but **I labored more abundantly than they all,** yet not I, but the **grace** of God which was with me (1 Corinthians 15:9-10).*

> *And God is able to make all **grace** abound toward you, that you, always having all sufficiency in all things, may have an abundance **for every good work** (2 Corinthians 9:8).*

*And He said to me, "My **grace** is sufficient for you, for My **strength** is made perfect in weakness." Therefore most gladly I will rather boast in my infirmities, that the **power of Christ** may rest upon me* (2 Corinthians 12:9).

*Therefore, since we are receiving a kingdom which cannot be shaken, let us have **grace, by which we may serve** God acceptably with reverence and godly fear* (Hebrews 12:28).

I think that a proper definition of grace coupled with a kingdom understanding of our commission—teaching them to obey all that I have commanded you—should stir our thinking toward the idea that grace is given to us so that we can obey God's commands. This is an almost 180 degrees different perspective from the conventional teaching on grace, which is mercy, lower standards, and God is nice. The law of God defines ungodliness, and the grace of God teaches and enables us to say no to it. We have often attributed to grace things that grace does *not* do, such as define sin and ungodliness—and not attributed to grace that which it *can do*, like help us accomplish our purpose on earth.

For the grace of God has appeared that offers salvation to all people. It teaches us to say "No" to ungodliness and worldly passions, and to live self-controlled, upright and godly lives in this present age (Titus 2:11-12 NIV).

Unconditional Love

A parallel problem exists with the concept of God's love. We are told God's love is unconditional. That means He loves you the same no matter what you do. It means He loves us all equally. That sort of means that at the reading of the will, all the children inherit equally. The idea that God is love and loves us, is so well-known in our society that, according to a *Macleans* magazine article, I read something like 80 percent of people in Canada, for example, think that when they die they will go to Heaven. Only a small percentage of Canadians are born again. Do the math. Maybe we have an imbalance in our perspective.

Unconditional love is one of those ideas that has a essence of truth but the packaging is misleading. It is good to know that God will still love us when we fail. Nothing can separate us from His love—not demons, not sin, not cable television. God does not give up on us. But at the same time, if we do not repent of our sins—get born again—before we die, we will go to hell. Hell is full of souls God loves unconditionally. To reap the rewards of what God has in store for those who believe is not unconditional. There is a condition. You must believe.

I risk belaboring this point, but our thinking is saturated with an unreal perception of God's love doing things for us that God never promised to do. We think that God's love for us is like a mother's love for her baby. Some moms continue to do laundry for their sons when they are 35 years of age. God is more like a father in that regard, "Here are some quarters. There's the laundromat."

Adam was kicked out of Paradise, and a big angel prevented him from sneaking back into the orchard to eat from the tree of life. He was cut off from *life*. He was never cut off from God's love. Jesus said, "I am the way the truth and the *life*" (John 14:6). "I have come that they may have *life*, and that they may have it more abundantly" (John 10:10). When did Jesus ever say that He came to give us love? To get God's life, we must do something. To get His life, we must obey His commands.

> *Blessed are those who **do** His commandments, that they may have the right to the tree of **life**, and may enter through the gates into the city* (Revelation 22:14).

To get God's love, we don't have to do anything. It's automatic. We dislike teaching or being taught about obeying God, so we teach the love of God and put emphasis there. Do I think that pastors are teaching love more than life because they seek to avoid the issues of obedience and standards? Yes, I do. Maybe not consciously, but the audience needs to be happy and pampered or they will go somewhere else.

Saint, get it into your heart that God loves you. Embrace that love. He loves you so much that He gave His *Huios* to die a horrible death on the cross for you. That proves irrefutably His love for you. Now get on with life. Embrace it. Grow up. Obey His commands. Enough already with unconditional and unmerited. They are adjectives. Let's get hold of some nouns.

What is love? What is favor?

When the New Testament speaks of God's love, it uses the Greek word *agape*. *Agape* means to do right toward another regardless of emotion. The right thing to do for a sinner when he dies is to put him in hell. God is going to do according to His love, and His love compels Him to do what is right. What is right or righteous is spelled out in the Bible and more specifically in the moral law. That is why love fulfills the law, because love does what is right and the moral law defines what is right. Love is not mindless sentiment or affection. Love for God is to obey His commands. Why? Obeying His commands causes us to do the right thing toward others regardless of emotion. That's what love is.

Hitting the Bull's-eye

We have looked at how the self-centered, somewhat immature view of church-centered theology has given us emphases and perspectives of concepts like grace that may be quite different from what they should be. The kingdom commission states that Jesus is Lord and King; and on that basis, we are to make disciples of all nations, teaching them to obey all that He commanded. That seems legalistic to us.

In present times, we produce *teknons*. The early church made disciples. There is a distinct difference. We bring people to a personal Savior. They declared the lordship of Christ. We hope it might be God's will to heal someone. They healed the sick. Peter's shadow healed more than we do. Or should I say, the average non-born-again person on the street in Peter's day had more faith in Peter's shadow to heal than members of the faith community have faith in God to heal today. This is not meant as criticism, but to show the need we have to mature into sonship.

Having the evangelical theology that puts justification at the center has caused us over time to redefine terms like grace and love. Imagine if all important Bible truth could placed on a dart board. We would want to put the most important in the bull's-eye. And then put the other truths around it. What is the central truth of the Word of God?

Let me expand on this. If the love of God is central, and by this I mean the common concept of love being affection rather than a commitment to do right regardless of emotion, we have a problem with hell. How can a loving God send anyone to hell? I am not as nice as God, and I would not choose to put people in an inferno for eternity. It's hard to reconcile a nice, loving God with the power He has condemning people to eternity in hell. Hell is not just a quick cremation and then you cease to exist. It's ongoing perpetual torment. People who have put the God of love in the bull's-eye interpret the Bible to adjust to this apparent dilemma. They come up with the idea that none will perish or they simply ignore certain Bible passages altogether.

Of course if you know that love is *agape*, a commitment to do right, the issue of hell can be better dealt with, but it is still problematic. Somehow to us it just never seems right to punish someone endlessly especially if their only crime was ignorance. Putting people in hell challenges our concept of His love.

If, on the other hand, the lordship of God is the central issue, then we have no argument with hell. The Lord is in charge; He does what He wants. Putting people in hell may challenge our concept of His love but it does not challenge our concept of His lordship. He made us. He can do whatever He wants. If I create a beautiful painting and you destroy it, then you are being evil; but if I destroy it, I am not being evil. It is mine to destroy should I choose to destroy it. Once a friend asked how I would feel if it turns out God is evil and not good. I responded that I don't serve God because He is good, I serve Him because He is God.

Kingdom theology sees the lordship of Jesus as the central truth of the Word of God. All other facets of God's nature are seen in the context of His lordship. I was teaching in Cornwall, England, one time on the lordship of God, and a pastor asked me, "What is a more important revelation, the love of God or the lordship of God?" Apparently in Great Britain at that time in many churches, the love of God was the emphasis and it was beneficial. I asked him what revelation Adam would have had considering that God gave him a command the first time He spoke to him.

Moses is the foremost and preeminent example of God giving revelation. Moses wrote the Pentateuch or the Torah. All other Scripture or revelation must agree with Moses, or it is discarded. Moses met with God at the burning bush. The first thing God said was, "Do not draw near. Remove your sandals" (Exod. 3:5). Those are commands. Then in the context of giving commands, God mentions that He is aware of the oppression of His people. That sounds like love. Then God tells Moses He is sending him to Egypt and that when he has brought the people out of Egypt, Moses will **serve** God on this mountain. So back to lordship. Then Moses asks God his name, and God says His *forever* name is LORD. The love of God, as vital and important as it is, must be seen within the context of His lordship.

> *Moreover God said to Moses, "Thus you shall say to the children of Israel: 'The **Lord**, God of your fathers, the God of Abraham, the God of Isaac, and the God of Jacob, has sent me to you. This is **My name forever**, and this is My memorial to all generations* (Exodus 3:15).

> *I appeared to Abraham, to Isaac, and to Jacob, as God Almighty, but by My name **Lord** I was not known to them* (Exodus 6:3).

If we put the Savior in the center of the dart board or personal salvation rather than the Lord, we end up with the evangelical perspective that Christianity is about what God can do for us rather than how we can serve God. Serving God is tainted by the perception that we are trying to earn salvation rather than accept the free gift. So we must remove salvation as the central tenant of faith and put the Lord in His rightful place as central. In this way, we can begin to see ourselves as servants and not be freaked out about it. We can journey toward *huios* on the only road provided. The road to greatness is to become a servant.

God's Perspective

To see ourselves as servants takes a bit of time and some adjustment. It might be helpful to confirm to our own thinking that God has a perspective that sees us as servants. Our first example is from an unlikely source, the Gospel of John. John is usually associated with the love of God.

> Then Pilate entered the Praetorium again, called Jesus, and said to Him, "Are You the King of the Jews?" Jesus answered him, "Are you speaking for yourself about this, or did others tell you this concerning Me?" Pilate answered, "Am I a Jew? Your own nation and the chief priests have delivered You to me. What have You done?" Jesus answered, "My kingdom is not of this world. If My kingdom were of this world, **My servants** would fight, so that I should not be delivered to the Jews; but now My kingdom is not from here." Pilate therefore said to Him, "Are you a king then?" Jesus answered, "You say rightly that I am a king. For this cause I was born, and for this cause I have come into the world, that I should bear witness to the truth..." (John 18:33-37).

Jesus thinks kingdom. He is the King and we are His servants. For this cause He came into the world.

> When they persecute you in this city, flee to another. For assuredly, I say to you, you will not have gone through the cities of Israel before the Son of Man comes. A disciple is not above his teacher, nor a servant above his master. It is enough for a disciple that he be like his teacher, and a servant like his master. If they have called the master of the house Beelzebub, how much more will they call those of his household! (Matthew 10:23-25)

We are the house or household; therefore, we are servants. The parable of the unforgiving servant from Matthew 18 teaches us that since we have been forgiven much, we should forgive our fellow servants. We understand from the way this story is told that Jesus is the King, and we are the servants. The parable of the wedding feast in Matthew 22 tells how the king sent out his servants to invite people to the feast. We understand it to mean that Christian workers must go out and preach the Word. God sees His workers as servants. In

Matthew 24, in the context of Jesus' return, He speaks the parable of the wise, faithful servant and the wicked servant. These are referring to His followers and again indicate that God sees us as servants. We know that the parable of the talents in Matthew 25 applies to us and again we are referred to as servants. The list goes on.

> *No servant can serve two masters; for either he will hate the one and love the other, or else he will be loyal to the one and despise the other. You cannot serve God and mammon* (Luke 16:13).

> *And which of you, having a servant plowing or tending sheep, will say to him when he has come in from the field, "Come at once and sit down to eat"? But will he not rather say to him, "Prepare something for my supper, and gird yourself and serve me till I have eaten and drunk, and afterward you will eat and drink"? Does he thank that servant because he did the things that were commanded him? I think not. **So likewise you,** when you have done all those things which you are commanded, say, "We are unprofitable servants. We have done what was our duty to do"* (Luke 17:7-10).

> *Most assuredly, I say to you, unless a grain of wheat falls into the ground and dies, it remains alone; but if it dies, it produces much grain. He who loves his life [soul] will lose it, and he who hates his life [soul] in this world will keep it for eternal life [zoe]. If anyone **serves** Me, let him follow Me; and where I am, there **My servant** will be also. If anyone **serves** Me, him My Father will honor* (John 12:24-26).

The pattern continues, and it becomes apparent that Jesus is comfortable calling us servants.

> *Let a man so consider us, **as servants of Christ** and stewards of the mysteries of God. Moreover it is required in stewards that one be found faithful* (1 Corinthians 4:1-2).

> *For he who is called in the Lord while a slave is the Lord's freedman. Likewise he who is called **while free is Christ's slave*** (1 Corinthians 7:22).

Tychicus, a beloved brother, faithful **minister** *[diakonos], and fellow* **servant** *[doulos] in the Lord, will tell you all the news about me* (Colossians 4:7).

Diakonos means minister, servant, or deacon; literally, one who labors in the dust. It is not as servile as a *doulos*. With *doulos*, the main thought is the relationship of dependence on the master. With *diakonos* it is on the service rendered. Tychicus was both servant and slave—as are we.

If you instruct the brethren in these things, you will be a good **minister** *of Jesus Christ, nourished in the words of faith and of the good doctrine which you have carefully followed* (1 Timothy 4:6).

When we affirm that we believe in Body ministry—that we are all ministers—we agree with God that we are in fact servants. By now I hope I have made a case for the concept that as born-again believers we are called to be servants. If you contend that point, I will not argue with you. I am not allowed to quarrel according to Second Timothy 2:24, "A servant of the Lord must not quarrel but be gentle to all, able to teach, patient." Throughout the Gospels and Epistles, we are referred to as servants. The last Book of the Bible is no exception, "…you allow that woman Jezebel, who calls herself a prophetess, to teach and seduce My *servants* to commit sexual immorality and eat things sacrificed to idols" (Rev. 2:20).

Repentance – a Change of Perspective

Our perspective of who God is must be adjusted to reflect the core issue of the Word of God—the lordship of Jesus. We must see God as Lord and Savior not just Savior. Our perspective of who we are must also be adjusted to align with God's perspective. We are servants. As unsavory as that may seem, we must adjust our thinking to it. We still have the challenges of 1) few if any clear role models and 2) how to go about being a servant, but we start up the right road when we embrace with our minds a theology that we are indeed servants.

The only proper way to serve the Lord is in the power of the Holy Spirit. *Christos* means the anointing. Christ in us is the Holy Spirit.

The kingdom of God is in the Holy Spirit, and we serve Christ in the strength His anointing provides. The idea that the Lord holds for us is not a grovelling slave in the dust but an anointed servant able to rule and reign in life. "I can do all things through Christ *which* strengtheneth me (Phil. 4:13 KJV). "Which" is used in the King James Version. "Who" is not used. I believe the verse is referring to the anointing of the Spirit not the Messiah, who as a person would require a personal pronoun. I can do all things through the anointing which empowers me.

Chapter Six

Anointed to Serve

I will put My Spirit within you and cause you to walk in My statutes... (Ezekiel 36:27).

"This is the new covenant I will make with My people on that day," says the Lord: "I will put My laws in their hearts [so they will understand them]*, and I will write them on their minds"* [**so they will obey them**] (Hebrews 10:16 NLT)

A correct understanding of the New Covenant includes that God wrote His laws in our hearts and minds and that He empowered us with the Holy Spirit to obey them. It has been said that you can not mix law and grace, but clearly from Scripture it is God's desired intent to do just that. This chapter looks at the importance of the anointing. God does expect us to obey, but He knows we cannot. We cannot fully obey in our own strength, but we can with His help. This chapter is about divine help.

To say we cannot obey in our own strength is not completely accurate since we can, to a degree, obey in our own effort. Many of us have experience wearing ourselves out doing just that. The Word tells us to make every effort, so I am not advocating a complete surrender to inactivity. What we are to do is make every effort to enter into His rest. Resting from our own labor and learning to work in His anointing is a job worth doing well.

Some might think that the anointing is for priests. In the Old Testament it seems that most of the time when the Lord spoke about the anointing, it was either on a priest, prophet, or a king.

What about ordinary people? We need to get hold of the fact that though we are ordinary saints, we are also priests and kings of the Lord. We are all ministers of the Lord and all need the anointing. We may not be called to pulpit ministry. We may be blue collar workers, those who work with our hands. Would it interest you to know that the first mention of the anointing was not on a priest or a prophet? It was on a craftsman. Call it the "craftsmen anointing," if you will. God imparted skill, wisdom, to a worker bee. That anointing is available for all.

The Craftsmen Anointing

*See I have called by name Bezalel the son of Uri, the son of Hur, of the tribe of Judah. And I have **filled him with the Spirit of God**, in wisdom, in understanding, in knowledge, and in all manner of workmanship* (Exodus 31:2-3).

The craftsmen anointing is mentioned in Exodus chapter 31. Bezalel was the first man in Scripture to be described as "filled with the Spirit of God." He was to build the Tabernacle and its furnishings. You are called to build the house of the Lord, the church. To do that you need the anointing. If you read Exodus 31, and I encourage you to do so, you will see that God basically took ordinary people and equipped them to serve Him. Just like in Ephesians 4:12 where we are told that the apostles and others are to equip the regular people to minister.

Please notice the second part of the chapter. Directly adjacent to the mention of the craftsmen anointing is instruction about the Sabbath. The church has various views about the Sabbath. It is one of the Ten Commandments that we have largely forgotten. It is the only one that starts off with the word "Remember." There's irony for you. God's instructions are pretty strict. Please read the following passage and see what I mean. Failure to obey the Sabbath resulted in death. God was adamant about this.

And the Lord spoke to Moses, saying, "Speak also to the children of Israel, saying: 'Surely My Sabbaths you shall keep, for it is a sign between Me and you throughout your generations, that *you may know that I am the Lord who sanctifies you. You shall keep the Sabbath, therefore, for it is holy to you. Everyone who profanes it shall surely be put to death; for whoever does any work on it, that person shall be cut off from among his people. Work shall be done for six days, but the seventh is the Sabbath of rest, holy to the Lord. Whoever does any work on the Sabbath day, **he shall surely be put to death**. Therefore the children of Israel shall keep the Sabbath, to observe the Sabbath throughout their generations as a perpetual covenant. It is a sign between Me and the children of Israel forever; for in six days the Lord made the heavens and the earth, and on the seventh day He rested and was refreshed"* (Exodus 31:12-17).

We should also read from Isaiah about Gentile converts who become servants of the Lord.

*Also the **sons of the foreigner** who join themselves to the Lord, to serve Him, and to love the name of the Lord, to be His servants—everyone **who keeps from defiling the Sabbath, and holds fast My covenant—even them** I will bring to My holy mountain, and **make them joyful** in My house of prayer. Their burnt offerings and their sacrifices will be accepted on My altar; for My house shall be called a house of prayer for all nations* (Isaiah 56:6-7).

And although the Evangelical church sees no reason to worry about the Sabbath, it seems that "the God who never changes" has some strong views. Personally, I find the Sabbath to be a delight (see Isa. 58:13). I started keeping the Sabbath (Saturday) over 18 years ago. I was pastoring at the time, and it always gave me a day of rest to wait on God before Sunday meeting. I don't worry about all the legalism attached with the Sabbath—I simply don't work for pay that day. I won't do my job, but I will minister to people in need. Eighteen years ago, many of my acquaintances thought I was nuts, but I am noticing that nowadays the Sabbath is becoming more respected. Anyway, like I said, God has some strong views about it. We may want to consider His point of view sometime, but for now I want to spiritualize the passage a bit.

I think we can glean from Exodus 31 that we seriously need the anointing to do God's work in the earth and we need to work out of *rest* or we will die. Some call it "burn out." God connects the thoughts of His anointing and the Sabbath because He wants us to work with His anointing and with His strength. We enter into rest when we humble ourselves before the Lord and get Him to work through us rather than trying to do it ourselves.

Humility is vitally important if we wish to become a *huios*. Moses was a man whom God humbled twice. Moses tried to deliver one Hebrew from an Egyptian. He did it in his own strength. He was called of God to rescue a nation, and perhaps he was just taking baby steps. After killing the horrible Egyptian, Moses had to get out of town. He spent 40 years in the wilderness learning he couldn't do it in his own strength. Then God appeared in the bush and gave Moses directions. It must have been frustrating for the Lord when Moses said he couldn't do it. Maybe 40 years had turned humility into low self-esteem. The fact is that Moses did hear from God and did eventually do what he was told. Then later, after leading the children out of Egypt, Moses had to spend another 40 years being humbled. Moses finally learned to operate out of rest.

Pride is the belief that we can do it in our own strength. It is often evidenced by a lack of prayer on the part of a minister. Remember, we are all ministers. A false image exists that some of us are ministers and others are just "regular people" who don't have to pray or serve in the anointing. Sorry, no such thing! No second class compartments in the kingdom. Pride is also the belief that we can't do it because we lack the strength, even though God says we can.

When the sons of Israel faced battle after coming out of Egypt, they rebelled against the Lord's instructions because of pride—we can't do it. Then later when they learned what the consequences were going to be for their lack of obedience, they tried to obey God in their own ability, without God's help. Both situations are evidence of pride.

To disobey God means we are trusting in our own ability to read a situation. We are pitting our pitiful wisdom against the wisdom of God and deciding we know better. That is pride. It was also unbelief in that they failed to understand after seeing the Lord work miracles, that God could fight with them against the Hittites. Pride fails to see God's strength. Humility sees our weakness, but it also sees His strength. God wants us to be humble.

> *And you shall remember that the Lord your God led you all the way these forty years in the wilderness, to **humble** you and test you, to know what was in your heart, whether you would keep His commandments or not. So He **humbled** you, allowed you to hunger, and fed you with manna which you did not know nor did your fathers know, that He might make you know that man shall not live by bread alone; but man lives by every word that proceeds from the mouth of the Lord* (Deuteronomy 8:2-3).

Forty years of eating manna was to teach the people of God humility. For 40 years God forced the Sabbath upon them by not sending manna on the Sabbath. This is a vital lesson for us today. We need not only see our limitations but also see the God who is more than enough. That's what entering into rest means to me. It means to relinquish control, to ask God for help, to listen to His instructions and to obey Him, believing that He is indeed capable. We let the anointing work. Once a friend told me that for years he worked for money, and now his money works for him. We need to stop laboring and let God's anointing work for us.

The craftsmen anointing is for us regular people to have wisdom to build the Body of Christ. We are to operate in that anointing and out of that anointing—not our own strength. We are to learn to operate out of rest. Next we will look at the healing anointing that Jesus gave to His followers and then the outpouring of anointing on the day of Pentecost.

The Matthew 10 Anointing

What is the Matthew 10 anointing? It is the authority and power to "do the stuff" as John Wimber used to say. Lord Jesus sent out the twelve and then the 70 (some Bible versions say 72). They experienced the anointing to heal and to preach. Then on the Day of Pentecost, the 120 were baptized in the Holy Spirit and received power from on high. The anointing spread and grew. Let's look at each of the three groups.

1. The Twelve

*And when He had called His twelve disciples to Him, **He gave them power over unclean spirits, to cast them out, and to heal all kinds of sickness and all kinds of disease*** (Matthew 10:1).

*Then He called His twelve disciples together and **gave them power** and **authority** over all demons, and to cure diseases* (Luke 9:1).

*These twelve Jesus sent out and **commanded** them, saying: "Do not go into the way of the Gentiles, and do not enter a city of the Samaritans. But go rather to the lost sheep of the house of Israel. And as you go, **preach**, saying, '**The kingdom** of heaven is at hand.' **Heal** the sick, **cleanse** the lepers, **raise** the dead, **cast out** demons. Freely you have received, freely **give**. Provide neither gold nor silver nor copper in your money belts, nor bag for your journey, nor two tunics, nor sandals, nor staffs; for a worker is worthy of his food"* (Matthew 10:5-10).

Please note the mention of preaching of the kingdom specifically, then healing and other supernatural signs, and finally the promise of provision. They are recurring themes.

2. The Seventy

And heal the sick there, and say to them, "The kingdom of God has come near to you" (Luke 10: 9).

Then the seventy returned with joy, saying, "Lord, even the demons are subject to us in Your name." And He said to them, "I saw Satan fall like lightning from heaven" (Luke 10:17-18).

Notice the same authority and power was given to the 70 as to the twelve to preach and to heal. They returned with joy.

Notice they were to do two things:

- Heal the sick (cast out demons, etc.). Part of deliverance/ healing is to deal with Ephesians 6:12 situations. Satan, the strongman, was bound, and his authority broken. Wickedness in heavenly places is cast down. Hence, Jesus saw satan fall.

- Preach that the kingdom of God is accessible here and now.

3. The One Hundred Twenty (Acts 1:15)

Behold, I send the Promise of My Father upon you; but tarry in the city of Jerusalem until you are endued with power from on high (Luke 24:49).

But you shall receive power when the Holy Spirit has come upon you; and you shall be witnesses to Me in Jerusalem, and in all Judea and Samaria, and to the end of the earth (Acts 1:8)

*When the Day of Pentecost had fully come, they were all with one accord in one place. And suddenly there came a sound from heaven, as of a rushing mighty **wind**, and it filled the whole house where they were sitting. Then there appeared to them divided tongues, as of **fire**, and one sat upon each of them. And they were all filled with the Holy Spirit and began to speak with other **tongues**, as the Spirit gave them utterance* (Acts 2:1-4).

*But Peter, standing up with the eleven, raised his voice and said to them, "Men of Judea and all who dwell in Jerusalem, let this be known to you, and heed my words. For these are not drunk, as you suppose, since it is only the third hour of the day. But this is what was spoken by the prophet Joel: 'And it shall come to pass in the last days, says God, that I will pour out of My Spirit on all flesh; Your **sons** [huios] and your daughters shall prophesy, your young men shall see visions, Your old men shall dream dreams. And on My **menservants** and on My **maidservants** I will pour out My Spirit in those days; and they shall prophesy"* (Acts 2:14-18. Note the mention of servants and that the anointing is for both genders).

They preached the kingdom and 3,000 souls were added to the church. Acts 2 has both preaching the kingdom and signs and wonders.

*Then Peter said to them, "**Repent,** and let every one of you be baptized in the name of Jesus Christ for the remission of sins; and you shall receive the gift of the Holy Spirit"* (Acts 2:38).

*Then fear came upon every soul, and **many wonders and signs** were done through the apostles* (Acts 2:43).

Acts 2:45 indicates provision as promised in Matthew 10:10. Acts 4 contains reference to both preaching and the persecution promised in Matthew 10:17. The number of the church grows to 5,000 men, plus women and children. After the persecution they prayed.

*And being let go, they went to their own companions and re-ported all that the chief priests and elders had said to them. So when they heard that, **they raised their voice to God with one accord** and said: "Lord, You are God, who made heaven and earth and the sea, and all that is in them, who by the mouth of Your servant David have said:'Why did the nations rage, and the people plot vain things? The kings of the earth took their stand, and the rulers were gathered together against the Lord and against His Christ.' For truly against Your holy **Servant** Jesus, whom You anointed, both Herod and Pontius Pilate, with the Gentiles and the people of Israel, were gathered together to do whatever Your hand and Your purpose determined before to be done. Now, Lord, look on their threats, and grant to Your ser-vants that with all boldness they may **speak Your word,** by stretching out Your hand **to heal, and that signs and wonders may be done through the name of Your holy Servant Jesus." And when they had prayed, the place where they were assem-bled together was shaken; and they were all filled with the Holy Spirit, and they spoke the word of God with boldness** (Acts 4:23-31).

"One accord" means everyone doing the same thing at the same time in the same place. They spoke the word of God with boldness. The Spirit in them was not a spirit of fear (see 2 Tim. 1:7) but of power. I'm thinking that the signs and miracles really helped boost their morales while they were out communicating among the peo-ple. In Acts 4:32-37, they shared possessions, which caused provi-sion. God provides. A pattern is apparent in Acts 1-6:

- Prayer

- Outpouring

- Preaching and healings

- Increase

- Provision

- Persecution

In Acts 6:3-8, more ministry is appointed.

> *Therefore, brethren, seek out from among you seven men of good reputation, full of the Holy Spirit and wisdom, whom we may appoint over this business;* **but we will give ourselves continually to [the]** *prayer and to the ministry of the word* (Acts 6:3-4. Note: Greek literally, "but we to the prayer and to the service of the word will keep." "**The** prayer" is likely a reference to prayer in the Spirit).

> *And the saying pleased the whole multitude. And they chose Stephen, a man full of faith and the Holy Spirit, and Philip, Prochorus, Nicanor, Timon, Parmenas, and Nicolas, a proselyte from Antioch, whom they set before the apostles; and when they had prayed, they laid hands on them. Then the word of God spread, and the number of* **the disciples multiplied greatly** *in Jerusalem, and a great many of the priests were obedient to the faith. And Stephen, full of faith and power, did* **great wonders and signs** *among the people* (Acts 6:5-8).

There are a few salient features in the overview of the Matthew 10 anointing:

1. They were to preach and heal (do miracles)—not just one or the other but *both*.

2. The number of those ministering increased—12-70-120—Joel seems to indicate "all" received the anointing.

3. Prayer is a vital component.

4. Provision seems to follow as they spread the power and message of the kingdom.

The preaching was to be about the currently accessible kingdom of God. Take special note of the content of what was actually recorded as being preached. Mark 6:12 says they preached that people should repent, but Matthew 10:7 says they were told to say the kingdom of God is at hand. Obviously, repentance is part of the kingdom preaching as written in Acts 2:38 and John 3:3-5.

The message of the kingdom has two important aspects. The kingdom of God is come in the now with an *outward* demonstration of power to heal sickness, cast out demons, and raise the dead. This includes supernatural power and provision for the believer and healing and salvation for the sinner. The second aspect of the kingdom is the governmental nature of it. This is more *internal* and has to do with accepting Jesus is Lord and Master of our lives and that we are His servants. We need to repent of sin and break off sin's control and submit to a new Master and Chief.

The best way to communicate the supernatural component of the message of the kingdom is to demonstrate it with signs and wonders. Then the Word needs to be preached with content that brings about conviction, contrition, and a confession of faith in the Lord with subsequent obedience (see Acts 6:7). This is why they were to heal *and* preach.

A second salient feature of the Matthew 10 anointing (as called in some circles), is that the ministry is not restricted to a select few. We see the anointing transferred to the twelve, then the 70, and later 120 were impacted. Later, we see new ministers appointed. One was Stephen who, as a deacon, did great signs and wonders among the people. Note carefully he did *great* signs and wonders. His signs and wonders were not just second-rate-deacon quality, but great. And he didn't do them in the church meetings but out among the people. Even Peter's shadow was capable of healing. Paul, who joined the party a little later, was doing signs and wonders, so apparently the miracle power of God is not diluted as greater numbers are equipped to minister.

A third salient point is that prayer is prominent. A time of prayer preceded both the day of Pentecost and the Acts 4:31 outpouring. They continued daily in the apostles' doctrine and prayer.

Of particular note is the mention in Acts 6:4 that the apostles would give themselves continually to *the* prayer and the ministry of the word. Some saints think the article "the" refers to a particular type of prayer, mainly praying in the Spirit, and it makes sense. Paul thanked God that he prayed in tongues "more than you all" (see 1 Cor. 14:18). It was a vital foundational component of his supernatural ministry.

When we pray in the Spirit, we activate spiritual edification and growth and pave the way in the spirit realm to accomplish things for the kingdom. We also need prayer to actively promote hearing from God. Hearing from God is an essential part of being His servant and knowing where to go and what to do.

Finally, it should be mentioned that God provided, as promised in Matthew 10. He warned them of coming persecution but also provided things such as money and food. This parallels the move of God in Egypt under Moses. There was preaching. There were signs and wonders. There was persecution and then provision as they took silver and gold and clothing from the Egyptians.

The Matthew 10 anointing is empowerment. It means we cast out demons, heal the sick, open blind eyes, and other signs and wonders. That it is currently available to you and me is definite. God is willing to impart if we are able to receive.

The Matthew 10 anointing is really part and parcel of being a *huios*. It is where we are going. It is what we want to embrace to further enable our becoming a *huios*. All of creation is eagerly waiting for the *huios* of God to manifest. A *huios* goes about doing good, healing all who are oppressed by the adversary.

A *huios* has embraced the fact that he or she started out as child of God by the act of the new birth. As a child they have matured and taken on the nature of the Father. God is love and love for God is that we obey His commands. Jesus, the *Huios* of God, demonstrated this by becoming a servant and being obedient even unto death on the cross. We, too, must follow this example. We must hear and obey the Spirit of God. Being a *huios* means embracing lordship as a way of life, but it also includes the ability to draw things like healings and miracles from the kingdom realm.

How do we get this Matthew 10 anointing? How do we activate it and walk in it? Do we travel to places where it is functioning? Do we invite in guest ministry? Do we read more books and listen to more tapes? Do we simply ask for it and step out and try it? Do we spend time praying in the Spirit—continually giving ourselves to *the* prayer? I think the answer is we do whatever it takes. We need this. We need to make every effort we can.

Adjuncts to the Matthew 10 Anointing

The following are additional insights into the ministry God expects of us, and we should expect from ourselves and our churches.

- We need a proper understanding of the kingdom of God and kingdom theology. Jesus is Lord as well as Savior. The law is a good thing and has been written in our hearts and minds. Knowing the covenant and knowing how to relate to a lord and master.

- A purposeful understanding in the *priesthood* of the believer and that the fivefold ministry has a job to equip the saints to do the work of the ministry. That means fivefold leaders or coaches should train the ordinary, everyday believer to do signs and wonders in the workplace and in homes. Ministry is not a paid position or office in an organization but the duty of every saint, every Christian— young or old, male or female, Jew or Gentile. Ministry takes us into the workplace and the community and may actually lead to evangelism and the opportunity to disciple new believers.

- Leadership that encourages this kind of ministry and is not threatened by it would be helpful. We need Holy Spirit-led leadership. We need gatherings that are structured to assist in developing maturity.

- A bonafide Holy Spirit baptism and active *prayer* life using our supernatural language complements our quest for maturity.

- A hunger for all that God has and an openness to learn new things (and really old things) and a willingness to repent of traditions of men that have hindered us from becoming a *huios*. A love and hunger for the Word.

Part II

Kingdom Foundations

Chapter Seven

The Kingdom Defined

"The secret of the kingdom of God has been given to you..."
(Mark 4:11 NIV).

I have been a Christian for 40 years and didn't really understand the kingdom of God for half of my Christian life. I sense I am not alone in this, for I have shared this teaching in churches in North America, Europe, Africa, and Asia and rarely find anyone who can clearly define the kingdom of God. This is in itself a kind of paradox.

> *Listen then to what the parable of the sower means: When any-one hears the* **message about the kingdom** *and does not* **under-stand** *it, the evil one comes and snatches away what was sown in his heart. This is the seed sown along the path. ...But the seed* [the message about the kingdom] *falling on good soil refers to someone who hears the word and* **understands** *it. This is the one who produces a crop, yielding a hundred, sixty or thirty times what was sown* (Matthew 13:18-23 NIV).

Understanding is key and understanding the kingdom of God will revitalize your Christianity and replace any weak footings with a solid foundation. Jesus said that if you don't understand the parable of the sower, then how can you understand any parable (see Mark 4:13). Since the parable of the sower centers on the message of the kingdom, it follows that if you don't grasp the meaning of the king-dom, you won't understand the parable either. This book is about un-derstanding.

Though it cost all you have, get understanding (Proverbs 4:7 NIV).

I discovered the meaning of the kingdom many years ago when I decided to take Matthew 6:33 seriously, "Seek ye first the kingdom of God." As I set out to seek the kingdom one morning, I realized that I didn't know what it was I was seeking. I had to ask the Lord what it was I was supposed to be seeking. For six months I researched the meaning of the kingdom of God and, for the most part, found out that authors and scholars wrote about the kingdom as if everyone knew what it was already. I did eventually find out what the kingdom is and began to make notes, thinking I would write a book. I didn't tell anyone about this at the time.

Doug Kelley, who was visiting our church in Canmore, prophesied to me that God wanted me to write a book, and that I had already started it, and that it would be about something others had written about but that it would have clarity of understanding to it. It has taken more than 11 years and a few rewrites, but here it is. May the Lord impart to you understanding as you about the kingdom.

*But **seek ye first the kingdom** of God, and His righteousness; and all these things shall be added unto you* (Matthew 6:33 KJV).

Kingdom Paradox

Define a paradox. (Please circle the letter corresponding to the best response.)

A. Mallard mates

B. Couple of surgeons

C. A statement seemingly absurd but in reality expressing a truth.

D. Two piers

The answer is, of course, C. (Mallard mates are a pair of ducks. A couple of surgeons are a pair of docs. Two piers are a pair of docks.)

The kingdom of God was central to the ministry of Jesus. He began His ministry by preaching "Repent for the kingdom of God is at hand" (Mark 1:15). The beatitudes start and finish with reference to the kingdom. The Lord's prayer says, "*Your kingdom come.*" Eighty percent of the parables teach about the kingdom. When He cast out demons, Jesus explained that it displayed the power of the kingdom. Jesus talked privately with both Nicodemus in John 3:3 and Pilate in John 18:33-19:12 about the kingdom. The disciples argued about who would be greatest in the kingdom. The thief on the cross asked Jesus to remember him when He came into His kingdom. Jesus told the disciples to preach the gospel of the kingdom (see Matt. 24:14) in all the world and then the end would come. He said that we would go through much tribulation to enter the kingdom. After His resurrection, Jesus spoke for 40 days with His followers about the kingdom of God (see Acts 1:3). Paul continued in the pattern.

He proclaimed the kingdom of God and taught about the Lord Jesus Christ—with all boldness and without hindrance! (Acts 28:31 NIV)

The Gospels are full of references to the kingdom of God. It is clearly the central theme. Unfortunately, there is a problem. Those of us who are to represent the kingdom of God on earth don't know what it is. We are king-dumb. Somehow this priority message in the Gospels has been obscured and lost to us.

The kingdom paradox is that the people called to represent the kingdom and to preach the kingdom, don't know what it is.

The Kingdom Defined

*For the kingdom of God is not a matter of eating and drinking, but of righteousness, peace and joy in the Holy Spirit, because anyone who **serves** Christ in this way is pleasing to God and receives human approval* (Romans 14:17-18 NIV).

The kingdom of God—synonymous with the kingdom of Heaven in Matthew's gospel—is not a place. It is not Heaven. It is not the church. A kingdom is a realm ruled by a monarch. Kingdom is translated from the Greek word *basileia* meaning royalty, rule or a realm, kingdom or reign. Ern Baxter defined the kingdom of God as the *government* of God. This makes sense. In that case, Matthew 6:33, *"seek ye first the kingdom of God,"* is saying, make it a priority to be governed by God.

The Lord's Prayer, "Thy kingdom come, Thy will be done," means, "Lord rule in my life today." The kingdom of God is simply the government or rule of God. It involves the volitional surrender of your will to God's will in which He becomes your Father and Master and you become his Son and Servant.

The Kingdom of God = the Government of God

We enter the kingdom of God when we, of our own free will, submit to the lordship of Jesus Christ. "That if you confess with your mouth the Lord Jesus and believe in your heart that God has raised Him from the dead, you will be saved" (Rom. 10:9). The kingdom of God is the government of God to which we volitionally surrender. We did this when we first believed, and we can continue to do it daily.

I have spoken in many various churches, house groups, Bible schools, and even seminaries about the kingdom of God, and rarely when I ask what they think the kingdom is do I get an appropriate or accurate answer. The one exception was when I was sharing in a house meeting in the north of London, England, in a place called Romford, Essex. An elderly Australian lady defined it as the *rule of Christ.* It was an amazingly good answer, so I initially thought this was a very informed group—until I found out she was a visitor that night.

Christ means the Anointing or the Anointed. It is a title that refers to Jesus as the Anointed or the Messiah. It also refers to the Holy Spirit, who is the Anointing or Christ in us.

Christ = the Anointing (Holy Spirit)

Christ = the Anointed (Messiah)

Jesus stands or sits at the right hand of God the Father. He is a resurrected Man, "For there is one God, and one Mediator between God and men, the Man [anthropos–human] Christ Jesus" (1 Tim. 2:5).

Jesus, the Man, does not live in our hearts physically. He lives there by His Spirit. So the Christ in us is the Holy Spirit.

We read in Romans 14:17 that the kingdom of God is *in* the Holy Spirit. The Holy Spirit is in us if we are indeed true disciples of Christ. We must allow the indwelling Spirit to govern us. "You, however, are controlled not by the sinful nature but by the Spirit" (Rom. 8:9 NIV 1984). The kingdom of God is the rule of the Holy Spirit. Being in the kingdom means allowing the Spirit to administer our lives instead of allowing sin to control us.

The Kingdom of God = the Rule of Christ

Now Matthew 6:33 really makes sense. Seek ye first the kingdom of God means make it a priority to be governed by the Holy Spirit. Let God be in control of your life. Let Jesus truly be Lord. It's a *daily* surrender. Now that we have defined the kingdom of God as the government of God or the rule of Christ, let's look at Romans 14:17-18 again.

The Kingdom Described: Righteousness, Peace, and Joy in the Holy Spirit

For the kingdom of God [rule of Christ or the government of God] *is not a matter of eating and drinking, but of righteousness, peace and joy in the Holy Spirit,* **because anyone who serves Christ** *in this way is pleasing to God and receives human approval* (Romans 14:17-18 NIV).

This passage is more of a description then a definition. The kingdom is not a matter of outward rules or rituals concerning what you can eat or drink. It is a matter of righteousness, peace, and joy in the Holy Spirit. It is a matter of serving Christ. The key is serving. We serve Christ by obeying Him.

Let's take a look at the three aspects: righteousness, peace, and joy.

1. **Righteousness.** The person under the government of God is not seeking to be justified. He is already justified. He is seeking to serve or please God as a blood-bought, Bible-taught, Spirit-filled,

flesh-killed, born-again disciple of the Lord Jesus. So we are not serving to be justified. We are serving because we *are* justified. We are not trying to earn sonship but to express sonship. This is important to establish, because it affects how we define righteousness.

Righteousness is both a gift and a fruit. We receive the gift of righteousness when we first confess Jesus as Lord and believe in our hearts that He is raised from the dead. This gift coupled with abundance of grace, allows us to reign in life (see Rom. 5:17). Jesus paid for this gift with His own blood on Calvary. It is by His blood, it is the work of Jesus, that makes us right before God. So faith in Jesus and His blood justifies, or makes us in right-standing or right-being, before God. Faith helps us see and enter the kingdom.

Justification equals the righteousness of right-standing with God and is a gift paid for by Jesus on Calvary and accepted by faith into the life of the believer. The fruit of righteousness is right-living or right-doing. It is also called sanctification. Justification is when you are legally set apart for God or made sacred or holy to Him.

Sanctification is the process of becoming holy in our behavior. It is the process of learning to live right or do right in God's eyes. It is the work of the Holy Spirit in us that sanctifies us. Therefore, since living under the rule of Christ is a matter of serving, it is principally concerned with the fruit of righteousness or right-living. Right-living springs or grows from right-standing. Sanctification is the process of learning appropriate behavior as a child of God. It is the work of the Holy Spirit and results as we by faith obey Him.

Right-doing equals doing right. Right is defined as anything that is the will of God. The will of God is revealed in the Word of God. Righteousness, or right-doing, is simply obedience to God. It is letting Jesus be our God-Lord-Master. We submit to the Word and the Spirit. What will happen to you if you bow your knee before God's throne? What will happen if you start to make a conscious effort to let Jesus control your life? First I'll tell you what Jesus won't do. He won't smack you on the head with a big stick, and say, "It's about time!" He will say, "Come up here and sit with Me, and we will rule together."

When we make Jesus King, then He makes us kings. I think it is to the degree that we let Jesus rule our lives that He lets us rule over the circumstances of life. As we come under authority, we are given authority. So the kingdom is not just about being governed by the Spirit and the Word, but about walking in the power and victory of the Spirit over sickness, spiritual darkness, financial problems, bondages, fears, and so on. It is reigning in life. It is walking according to love.

> *For if by the one man's offense death reigned through the one, much more those who receive abundance of grace and of the gift of righteousness will **reign in life** through the One, Jesus Christ* (Romans 5:17).

Love is fulfilling the law and obeying His commands. "This is love for God: to obey His commands" (1 John 5:3 NIV 1984). "Love is the fulfillment of the law" (Rom. 13:10 NIV). Some of us think that "love is the fulfillment of the law" means that if we would just love one another we would automatically fulfill the law. In some respects, that is true. It depends on our connotation of love. If we have a weak or insufficient understanding of love, then we won't fulfill the law. The law defines how loves acts so that we know what loves is. First John 5:3 makes it clear that God is not leaving the definition of love up to us. He tells us with no uncertainty what love is. It is to obey His law, or His commands.

As mentioned previously, the Greek word for love is *agape*. *Agape* means a commitment to do right for another regardless of emotion. It is a commitment to do what God says to do in the Word. Both righteousness and love fulfill the will or law of God. They are related.

2. Peace is more than the absence of anxiety. It means nothing missing, nothing broken. It means health and wholeness, prosperity and success in the things of God. Peace relates to covenant and includes all the benefits of the cross—listed at the end of this chapter.

Peace is a gift and a fruit. "My peace I give to you," Jesus said in John 14:27. When we first trusted in Jesus, we were given peace with God (see Rom. 5:1). There is also the peace of God (see Phil. 4:6-7). Peace comes from obeying the Prince of Peace (see Isa. 9:6-7). Peace is fruit, "But the fruit of the Spirit is love, joy, peace..." (Gal. 5:22).

The peace mentioned in Romans 14:17 is fruit. Notice the similarity between Romans 14:17 and Galatians 5:22.

Rom. 14:17 Government of God	Righteousness = Doing right	Peace	Joy
Gal. 5:22 Fruit of the Spirit	Love = Commitment to do right	Joy	Peace

3. Joy is a gift and a fruit as well. Joy is associated with:

a) Prayer as in John 16:24 and Isaiah 56:7 "...these I will bring to My holy mountain and *give them joy* in My house of prayer..." (NIV).

b) Witnessing as in Psalm 51:12-13 and Luke 10:17.

c) The presence of God, "You will fill me with joy in Your presence" (Ps. 16:11 NIV); "in Thy presence is fulness of joy" (Ps. 16:11 KJV).

d) Strength, "The joy of the Lord is your strength" (Neh. 8:10). God gives us His joy so we can serve Him with His strength. Joy also speaks of the benefit of simply knowing God, the beauty of having sins forgiven, and the hope we have for the future. We cannot serve Christ in our own strength—only by His grace. God resists the proud, self-sufficient, but gives grace to the humble. Serving God is to be a joy not a burden (see Deut. 28:47-48). To serve God joyfully means we need to be constantly filled with the Holy Spirit.

I mentioned earlier that I used to teach on the kingdom of God. I would ask people to define it and rarely got a good answer except from the Australian saint. Commonly I would get the phrase righteousness, peace, and joy in the Holy Spirit, which isn't a definition. It sounds spiritual and scriptural, but it doesn't mean the person giving this answer has a clue as to what it means.

Now that we have defined the kingdom and unpackaged what righteousness, peace, and joy are, I hope you have a better idea of what exactly the kingdom of God is. Now if you read the Gospels again with a kingdom focus, look at the many parables of the kingdom and interpret them with this new information.

I remember back before I had studied out the meaning of the kingdom how it seemed that many books just assumed you knew what the kingdom was. But for me it was vague and maybe for you, too. Now armed with a clear idea that kingdom means government or rule, we can look at other aspects of divine truth such as the new birth and the covenant and begin to see them more accurately. Let's look briefly at the New Covenant.

Righteousness, Peace, and Joy Relate to Covenant

For this is the covenant that I will make with the house of Israel after those days, says the Lord: **I will put My laws in their mind and write them on their hearts; and I will be their God, and they shall be My people** (Hebrews 8:10).

...As God has said: "I will live with them and walk among them, and I will be their God, and they will be My people" (2 Corinthians 6:16 NIV).

I said that peace relates to covenant, actually all three elements—righteousness, peace, and joy—relate to covenant. God's covenant can be expressed as three statements:

"I will be your God."
"You will be My people."
"I will be with you."

"I will be your God" means God gets to be God. He is the authority. He is the Lord. We declare his lordship as we are being born again. His laws are written in our hearts and minds. We follow His laws, teachings, and commandments. *"You will be My people"* means we have access to all covenant blessings including salvation, peace, health, prosperity, and wisdom. It speaks of the benefits of relationship

and sonship. We reign in life through one Man, Christ Jesus. *"I will be with you"* means the continual blessing of His presence in which there is fullness of joy. This joy is our strength.

A disciple of Jesus Christ has God's law written in his heart and in his mind. He walks under the government of God, according to the covenant that we have with God. To know how to be ruled by the Spirit, we need to know the covenant or testament—both Old and New Testaments.

Disciples of the King understand that they enjoy special privilege with God and a special responsibility before God. We know God for who He really is—LORD (see Heb. 8:11), and we treat Him accordingly. The government of God, or the rule of Christ expressed as righteousness, peace, and joy, relates to these three aspects of covenant.

**Disciples of Jesus Christ have God's
law written in their hearts and minds.
They walk under the government of God
according to the covenant.**

Covenant	Kingdom of God
I will be your God	Obedience to God: Righteousness
You will be My people	Enjoying the benefits of being God's child: Peace
I will be with you	The ongoing presence of God: Joy

Entering the kingdom of God is coming under Jesus' government. We submit to His lordship and learn His ways. He initially gives us right-standing with Him and then empowers us with the Spirit to produce the fruit of right-living. Through the obedience of faith, we come under His authority and learn of Him. Then we can exercise authority. We can enjoy all the benefits of sonship. He promises that He will be with us always. His joy and the privilege of His intimate fellowship strengthen us.

Benefits of the Cross

Bless the Lord, O my soul, and forget not all His benefits (Psalm 103:2).

Derek Prince wrote an excellent series years ago on the foundation stones of the faith. If memory serves, then I should credit Derek Prince with the following notes. These benefits are really worth remembering. At a recent Huios House meeting, my wife wanted to review them as we worshiped. Please spend some time learning these benefits.

1. Jesus was punished that we might be *forgiven.*

2. Jesus was wounded that we might be *healed.* Isaiah 53:4-5 reveals that Jesus bore the consequences of our sin both on the spiritual and physical planes. Our sins are forgiven and our sickness is healed (see 1 Pet. 2:24).

3. Jesus was made sin with our sinfulness that we might become *righteous* with His righteousness, "For He [God] made Him [Jesus] who knew no sin to be sin for us, that we might become the righteousness of God in Him" (2 Cor. 5:21).

4. Jesus died our death that we might share His *life.* Jesus tasted death for everyone. See Hebrews 2:9 and Romans 6:23.

5. Jesus became poor with our poverty that we might become *rich* with His riches, "that you through His poverty might become rich" (2 Cor. 8:9 NIV). While Jesus walked this earth, He was not poor. He had all that He needed to do the will of God in His own life. But on the cross, Jesus was hungry, thirsty, naked, in need, and had to be buried in a borrowed tomb. (See also Second Corinthians 9:8.)

6. Jesus bore our shame that we might share His *glory.*

7. Jesus endured rejection that we might have His *acceptance* as children of God. See Matthew 27:46,50. Jesus suffered rejection and shame for us. "Jesus...endured the

cross, despising the shame" (Heb. 12:2); "bringing many sons to glory" (Heb. 2:10); "He made us accepted in the beloved" (Eph. 1:5-6 KJV).

8. Jesus became a curse that we might receive a *blessing*, "Christ has redeemed us from the curse of the law...that the blessing of Abraham might come upon [us]" (Gal. 3:13-14).

When Jesus had accomplished all this for us on the cross, He said, "It is finished." The blessing of Abraham comes to us. Bless means to empower, to prosper—spiritually, socially, physically, and financially. So in the kingdom context, peace means all these things.

Chapter Eight

The New Birth Redefined

This chapter is called The New Birth Redefined rather than just defined. We are used to operating with certain terminology and religious jargon. We take for granted that words and expressions mean things but fail to comprehend that they meant something differently centuries ago in cultures quite distinct from our own. We are remiss when we interpret the Bible in light of our own culture or context. An example of this could be "born of water" from John 3:5:

> *Jesus answered, "Most assuredly, I say to you, unless one is born of water and the Spirit, he cannot enter the kingdom of God."*

We wonder, What does born of water mean? Then we think, Ah yes, when a woman gives birth, her water breaks. This is what is meant by born of water. Makes sense right? Only one problem, the ancient cultures (both Greek and Hebrew) didn't describe it that way. The language of the New Testament is Greek, as you know, so maybe born of water was a common Greek expression. No. The Greeks didn't use that expression in any of their writings to describe a mother's water breaking. The Jews used the expression for the ritual cleansing of dipping in water. Born of water had no relationship to a mother's water breaking in Jewish culture, but it meant immersion in water for cleansing. This gives some light to John 3:5.

Have you been under the impression that born of water meant the mother's water breaking? Do you see that it is possible that we have introduced our own cultural interpretations into the Scriptures? Do you want to have some of those cultural misinformations clarified? Well, then let us proceed with an openness and willingness to have some of our thinking renewed.

New Birth

One enters the kingdom of God, or the rule of Christ, through a process called the new birth. You could say that being born again is *coming under new management* or being digitally remastered. Too often we have equated being born again with being saved and have not considered the component of government. In fact, because it's so prevalent to consider the new birth synonymous to salvation, I must diffuse any potential misunderstanding.

Salvation can mean "safe from hell." I'm glad to be safe from hell. One of the things that motivated me to explore the claims of Christ was the suspicion that hell might exist. We know that whosoever calls on the name of the Lord shall be saved (see Acts 2:21; Rom. 10:13). If you are a sinner dying in a car accident and call on Jesus with your last remaining gasps, you can be forgiven and go to Heaven. In that instance, you were saved from hell. You were saved from the consequences of your sin, but you died before you had the opportunity to grow as a child of God. Your "by the skin of your teeth" escape hardly qualifies as experiencing kingdom life—righteousness, peace, and joy. You never really became a disciplined follower of Jesus.

Salvation has another meaning, "salvaged from sins." Jesus came to save us from our sins (see Matt. 1:21) not just the consequences of sin. The apostles and early disciples would have understood salvation this way. (For more details about this, consult *The Normal Christian Birth* by Davis Pawson.) They saw salvaging us from sins here in this life as a process, not as fire insurance for the afterlife. We are given salvation as a free gift, but we work out that salvation with fear and trembling.

Because the safe-from-hell connotation of salvation is so strong in our thinking, I want to separate the new birth from salvation, for a moment, and give it a different association. I want to develop its kingdom or governmental context.

*Now there was a man of the Pharisees named Nicodemus, a member of the Jewish ruling council. He came to Jesus at night and said, "Rabbi, we know You are a teacher who has come from God. For no one could perform the miraculous signs You are doing if God were not with Him." In reply Jesus declared, "I tell you the truth, no one can **see the kingdom** of God unless he is born again." "How can a man be born when he is old?" Nicodemus asked. "Surely he cannot enter a second time into his mother's womb to be born!" Jesus answered, "I tell you the truth, no one can **enter the kingdom** of God unless he is born of water and the Spirit"* (John 3:3-5 NIV 1984).

Jesus said, "I tell you the truth, no one can see the kingdom of God unless he is born again." Please note Jesus did not say, "I tell you the truth, no one can be saved unless he is born again." **The subject is *not* salvation.** It is the kingdom. In fact, it is about **"seeing" the kingdom.** Jesus was saying no one can get a revelation of the government of God unless he is born again. We first need to see the government of God.

Then Jesus said, "I tell you the truth, no one can *enter* the kingdom of God unless he is born of water and the Spirit." Again He is talking about the kingdom not salvation per se. This time He is focusing on *entering* the kingdom. So there is a seeing and a subsequent entering the government of God. It is like when you come to a doorway. You can see into the room and then you can enter the room. First the kingdom is revealed and then realized. So the new birth is about the government of God. It is about seeing and entering it.

Being born again starts when you hear the Word of God preached and conviction touches your heart, "For you have been born again...through the living and enduring word of God" (1 Pet. 1:23 NIV). Faith comes by hearing the Word of God. We accept the message of the gospel which calls us to repent. We repent and believe in the Lord Jesus. That, simply put, is the beginning of a new life. According to Jesus, you are now at the stage where you can see the government of God or the rule of Christ. You haven't entered it yet. You enter the rule of Christ by being born of water and the Spirit.

Now if what I am saying about the new birth is accurate, then we should see something in the New Testament that shows the disciples doing what I am describing. Jesus commissioned His followers to go and make disciples. A disciple of Christ has recognized and accepted the lordship of Jesus. He is under new management, an apprentice. We make disciples by baptizing them and by teaching them to obey all that Jesus commanded.

> *Then Jesus came to them and said, "All authority in heaven and on earth has been given to Me. Therefore go and make disciples of all nations, baptizing them in the name of the Father and of the Son and of the Holy Spirit, and teaching them to obey every- thing I have commanded you. And surely I am with you always, to the very end of the age"* (Matthew 28:18-20 NIV).

If a disciple is an apprentice of Jesus, submitted to His leadership, under His government, then there must be a connection between being born again and becoming a disciple. Jesus does not commission us to simply preach good news and have people make decisions but to make disciples. Let's take a closer look at His commission.

His Commission

All authority in heaven and on earth has been given to Me: This statement is a declaration of the lordship of Jesus Christ. He is, in fact, saying I AM God. He is stating His sovereignty. Many people forget this part of the commission. This is a kingdom statement. The great commission is stated in a kingdom context. *Therefore go and make disciples of all nations:* "Therefore" alludes back to the first statement. In other words, He is saying, because I am sovereign, go and tell people in all ethnic groups. Make them My disciples. Let them know Me for who I am, LORD. Make them subjects of My rule by *baptizing them* [immersing them in water] *in the name of the Father and of the Son and of the Holy Spirit.*

And teaching them to obey: What are we to teach new believers to obey? The new covenant is about the Lord writing His laws on the tablets of our hearts and minds. We could teach that and everything else Jesus commanded us. It sounds like Jesus is under the impression that He is in charge. He is saying, go and teach people to obey My commands. Apparently we are supposed get them to come under God's government. *And surely I am with you always, to the very end of the age:* is the promise of His empowering presence. It is the promise of enduring joy and strength.

Peter understood the meaning and context of Matthew 28:18-20. He stood up on the day of Pentecost and declared the lordship of Jesus Christ. The people responded to the gospel of the kingdom by asking what they must do. Peter instructed them as follows: Repent and be baptized, in the name of Jesus Christ for the forgiveness of your sins. And you will receive the gift of the Holy Spirit. He told them, in effect, to be born of water and the Spirit.

> *"Therefore let all Israel be assured of this: God has made this Jesus, whom you crucified, both Lord and Messiah." When the people heard this, they were cut to the heart and said to Peter and the other apostles, "Brothers, what shall we do?" Peter replied, "**Repent and be baptized**, every one of you, in the name of Jesus Christ for the forgiveness of your sins. And you will receive the gift of the **Holy Spirit**"* (Acts 2:36-38 NIV).

Jesus told Nicodemus that in order to *enter* the kingdom, to submit to the rule of Christ, he must be born of water and the Spirit. Water baptism was symbolic of dying to the old life and starting anew with old sins removed. Water baptism is also the first outward step of obedience that a new believer takes. In order to come under new government, the person must first die to the old.

Second, in order to operate in the kingdom, under God's government, you need to be empowered with divine enablement. You need the Spirit spoken of in Ezekiel 36:26-27 (NIV):

> *I will give you a new heart and put a new spirit in you; I will remove from you your heart of stone and give you a heart of flesh. And I will put My Spirit in you and **move you to follow my decrees** and be careful to keep My laws.*

Since we cannot operate in the kingdom without the Holy Spirit, it follows that part of the process involved in entering that domain would be to receive the Spirit. His purpose in giving the Spirit is clear. It is so we can obey His laws.

The new birth described in John 3:3-5 must be understood in the context of the kingdom of God. Since the kingdom of God is the government of God, the new birth must be seen as the passage from self-rule, sin's control, and the domain of satan, the old government, to the rule of Christ, the new government, and not simply a synonym for being saved. A careful comparison of Jesus' conversation with Nicodemus and His commission to His followers, including the way those followers applied His commission, verifies this conclusion and interpretation. The new birth is not fire insurance. It is a chance to live as a son of God—free of sin's control.

The New Birth Process

Natural birth is a process. When the baby is ready to be born, it turns, so that its head faces toward the birth canal. Then, as the mother has contractions, the baby moves down the birth canal from the dark quiet of the womb into the light of the hospital or birthing room. In the next few moments, the baby's umbilical cord is severed and the baby will breathe. The baby goes from one form of life support to another. After this, the baby is usually cleaned and placed next to the mother to be cuddled or fed.

The new birth is also a process. A person coming to Christ must turn toward God. He must believe in the Lord Jesus as he passes from the darkness to the light. His old life support must be severed in water baptism. He must breathe in the Holy Spirit. Then he must be cleaned, loved, nurtured, and discipled.

There are four essential steps in the actual birth itself. These four things are foundational in the life and faith of a new believer. The four steps are:

1. Repentance

2. Faith toward God

3. Water baptism

4. Being filled with the Holy Spirit (see Heb. 6:1-2)

These steps will be explained in some detail because of their extreme importance. I must remind you at this point that the new birth is a process of a change of government. Please keep that in mind. When someone comes to Christ, he or she is not just buying a ticket to Heaven. It is a major change of life similar to marriage.

Marriage is a process. First, contact is made between two people (or two families, as is the case in some Eastern cultures). In the course of time, there is growing affection, or negotiations that transpire. Then the two become engaged or betrothed to be married—a decision has been made. After this, there is a wedding ceremony in which the decision to marry is formally and publicly recognized and ratified. Subsequent to the nuptials is the very private act of intercourse that consummates the marriage. At what point in the process is one considered married?

If you have a formal ceremony but do not consummate the marriage, then it is not legal. Conversely, if you consummate without a wedding, then it is fornication, not marriage. It also stands to reason that if you decide not to marry, then you won't. All the parts of this process are essential to arrive at the finished product. Both the illustrations of marriage and natural birth depict accurately what happens in the new birth.

Repentance is like when the baby turns toward the birth canal or like the decision to date or be betrothed. Faith in Christ is like coming into the light, such as when the baby is born or like the formal decision to marry. Water baptism is the severing of the umbilical cord or the public wedding ceremony. Water baptism, severing the umbilical cord, and the wedding ceremony are all things that occur only once. Finally the baby breathes (breath = *pnema*, which also means spirit) or the marriage is consummated by intercourse. These speak of being filled with the Holy Spirit. Like breathing or intercourse, being filled happens continually through out your life—or marriage.

The four initial steps of seeing and entering the Rule of Christ	
1. Repentance from acts leading to death 2. Faith in the Lord Jesus Christ	Seeing
3. Immersion in water 4. Being filled with the Holy Spirit	Entering

Chapter Nine

Seeing the Kingdom

The new birth or being born again into the kingdom of God involves four steps. The first two have to do with seeing the kingdom. Let me remind you that we are discussing the kingdom not salvation. To be saved, a person must call on the Lord. To see the kingdom, a person must repent and believe.

Repentance

Repentance and faith are linked to seeing the kingdom of God. Repentance is our English word translated from a Greek word *metanoia* meaning to perceive afterward. It is a function of perception. Basically, one could say repentance is seeing something in hindsight or in the context of relating to God, from God's point of view. When merged with the Hebrew understanding of repentance, we could accurately define repentance as a change of perception that leads to a change in behavior. Repentance is more than saying, "I'm sorry." The key verse for repentance is as follows:

> ...I preached that they should repent and turn to God and prove their repentance by their deeds (Acts 26:20 NIV).

We repent of sins. Imagine expecting new converts to **prove** their repentance. Does anyone do that nowadays? One of the problems we encounter today stems from a simplistic concept of repentance that says we can pray a general prayer like, "Forgive me for my sins" or "I confess that I am a sinner." This shotgun approach does not help us change. Vague concepts of sin and vague confessions don't lead to action; whereas specific confessions focus on where the action needs to take place. Better to say to your spouse, "Sorry, honey, that I ridiculed you in front of your friend. In the future I will try not to make jokes at your expense," than to say, "Sorry, honey, I think I said something that upset you." We need to clearly define what sin is.

> *I would not have known what sin was except through the law* (Romans 7:7 NIV).

Sin can be generally defined as anything against God and specifically defined as breaking the commandments of the law. The moral law of God reveals sins, "On the contrary, I would not have known what sin was except through the law" (Rom. 7:7 NIV). But there is something even more basic than breaking the rules. It is failing to acknowledge the ruler. Many people simply fail to recognize God for who He is. They have not only failed to obey His commands, but they have forgotten who He is, or made Him out to be different from who He is, or denied His existence.

This is why we so desperately need repentance. The law not only reveals the rules but also the character and nature of God. We need to see Him as He is. We need a change of perception. He is Lord. He knows what is best. He has every right to rule. As we wrap our thinking around that concept, we will begin to align ourselves, our souls, and our lifestyles to that lordship. As we begin to see God correctly, we will start to seek His government. This repentance is the initial step in seeing the kingdom of God.

Repentance means to turn from evil practices to reformed ways and actions that are in accordance with God's decrees. (Turn is translated in the New Testament as be converted.) The opposite of this is to continue with our own plans, agenda, and remain stubborn. Repentance to the Jewish disciples of Christ was not just a decision confined to the mind. It meant to stop doing one thing and to do another. It was an action, or in other words, a lifestyle change, faith proved by works. They had to prove their repentance by their deeds (see Acts 26:20).

> *When he finally came to his senses, he said to himself, "At home even the hired servants have food enough to spare, and here I am dying of hunger! I will go home to my father and say, 'Father, I*

have sinned against both heaven and you, and I am no longer worthy of being called your son. Please take me on as a hired servant'" (Luke 15:17-19 NLT).

There are three parts to repentance: the inward, the visible, and the audible (thought, action, and word). The prodigal son realized (came to his senses) that he had sinned (notice that he realized that he had sinned against his father and against Heaven, God). He had hurt God by wasting his life. He got up and went (action). He spoke to his father (audible).

Repentance (see Heb. 6:1) is from acts that lead to death.

Repentance involves three things:

1. Thinking differently. We hear the truth and let it change our point of view.

2. Speaking differently. The words we speak are important. "For by your words you will be acquitted, and by your words you will be condemned" (Matt. 12:37 NIV see also Mark 7:18-23 and James 3:9-10). "Confess your sins to each other" (James 5:16 NIV). We verbally confess our sins (sins, plural, see Matt. 1:21). It is important to confess specific sins not just general sin. Naming our sins kills our pride. By confessing sin in general now, we may end up glossing over specific things later by assuming that they were covered already in the general confession. Vague confessions don't lead to much action, whereas specific confession focuses where the action needs to take place.

Repentance is an ongoing process. You won't deal with all your sins in one go. God seems to focus on one or two areas at a time. Joshua took the Promised Land bit by bit. It is also important to be convicted of a sin before we confess it. Just like faith comes by hearing the message, repentance follows an understanding of truth. Truth and the Spirit of Truth, the Holy Spirit, work together to produce conviction. In leading others to Christ, we, the church, have used the old sales ploy of strike while the iron is hot. We have put too much emphasis on going to Heaven and avoiding hell and on making a decision for Christ based on that little bit of info. We need to take time to tell the truth. Jesus is the Truth. Let's take time to tell people about Jesus—who He is, what He is like, how much He loves us, why He is LORD. Testify of Him. In the light of who Jesus is, we see our need to repent.

3. Acting differently.

> *Jesus entered Jericho and was passing through. A man was there by the name of Zacchaeus; he was a chief tax collector and was wealthy. He wanted to see who Jesus was, but because he was short, he could not see over the crowd. So he ran ahead and climbed a sycamore-fig tree to see Him, since Jesus was coming that way. When Jesus reached the spot, He looked up and said to him, "Zacchaeus, come down immediately. I must stay at your house today." So he came down at once and welcomed him gladly. All the people saw this and began to mutter, "He has gone to be the guest of a sinner." But Zacchaeus stood up and said to the Lord, "Look, Lord! Here and now I give half of my posses-sions to the poor, and if I have cheated anybody out of anything, I will pay back four times the amount." Jesus said to him, "Today salvation has come to this house, because this man, too, is a son of Abraham. For the Son of Man came to seek and to save what was lost"* (Luke 19:1-10 NIV).

When Zacchaeus saw Jesus, he repented. It is interesting that in this passage, salvation is the result of a confession of repentance alone. In other passages it appears that salvation is the result of faith alone or faith and baptism together. It is important not to base our doctrine on only one verse. This verse may not mean that repentance is the only thing needed for salvation, but it certainly shows a rela-tionship between repentance and salvation.

After we have named specific sins, we need to take responsibility. No excuses. If we stole ten dollars, we need to tell whoever it was we stole from that we stole it. Take responsibility. Then we need to make restitution. That means we pay the money back. (Actually according to the Old Testament we should pay back with interest.) And then we need to renounce the sin.

Renounce means to abandon the practice, decline association with it, withdraw from it. Stop stealing. You may have to clean house. Repentance costs something. "A number who had practiced sorcery brought their scrolls together and burned them publicly.

When they calculated the value of the scrolls, the total came to fifty thousand drachmas" (Acts 19:19 NIV). They renounced witchcraft. Do you need to renounce anything?

Repentance is a gift from God. God enables us to see a divine perspective. It follows instruction.

> *God exalted Him* [Jesus Christ] *to His own right hand as Prince and Savior that He might give repentance and forgiveness of sins to Israel* (Acts 5:31 NIV 1984).

> *And the Lord's servant must not be quarrelsome but must be kind to everyone, able to teach, not resentful. Opponents must be gently instructed, in the hope that **God will grant them repentance** leading them to a knowledge of the truth, and they will come to their senses and escape from the trap of the devil, who has taken them captive to do his will* (2 Timothy 2:24-26 NIV).

Repentance is the responsibility of man. It is a response that God expects of people who are confronted with truth. God "commands all people everywhere to repent" (Acts 17:30 NIV). Responding to God's truth, through repentance, brings blessing. Ignoring God has serious consequences. Fortunately for us, God is patient.

God "is patient with you, not wanting anyone to perish, but everyone to come to repentance" (2 Pet. 3:9 NIV). From the context of this Scripture, it would seem that the alternative to coming to repentance is to perish. To perish in this context means to burn in the coming judgment of God. Ultimately, if we, or anyone for that matter, continue to ignore God, the full consequences will have to be met. People who choose not to respond to God's truth have by default chosen to follow satan and his lies. They will end up following satan to the judgment God has prepared for him. We can be saved from that judgment by repenting.

> *When the people heard this, they were cut to the heart and said to Peter and the other apostles, "Brothers what shall we do?" Peter replied, "**Repent and be baptized**, everyone of you, in the name of Jesus Christ for the forgiveness of your sins..."* (Acts 2:37-38 NIV).

Repentance is the thought process when we reflect on truth and change our perceptions to bring them in line with that truth. It is a process that will initiate our becoming a believer in Christ. It is a process we will subscribe to throughout our Christian life if we desire to grow in Christ. Repentance is a prerequisite to our faith in God. It is also sort of a co-requisite since we would probably not repent if we didn't have some belief in Jesus. If our faith in God is not founded upon true repentance, then we will have a man-made faith, which may account for the variety and number of alternate religions. True faith in God is not based on our own ideas but on God's truth. Repentance is that step where we allow His truth to change our way of thinking so that it will reflect His way of thinking.

Complete repentance is a change of mind that we verbalize and act upon. It is completed when we take full responsibility for our sins, make restitution for any damages we caused, and renounce the activity in which we were involved. This change of mind leads to a change of heart and lifestyle. Repentance turns us away from sins, and faith turns us toward God. This change of heart can be called conversion. Conversion means to do a U-turn (see Mark 4:12). Conversion is like the visible portion of repentance coupled with believing. Conversion is to turn away from a self-centered, sinful life as a result of repentance and to turn to God with faith in Jesus Christ.

> *Repent, then, and **turn to God** [be converted or convert yourselves], so that your sins may be wiped out, that times of refreshing may come from the Lord, and that He may send the Messiah, who has been appointed for you—even Jesus* (Acts 3:19-20 NIV).

It should be noted that although we must convert—conversion is our responsibility—to become followers of Christ, He wants disciples not just converts.

There is *initial repentance* when we first come to Christ. We need to repent of the specific sins in our lives. Take time with seekers— pre-believers, prospects, sinners—to explain repentance. We repent to the **Father**. We tell Him we are sorry about hurting Him, rebelling against Him, and taking His love for granted. We commit to obedience in the future and to make things right with people we have wronged.

There is also *ongoing repentance* as God convicts us of sin. It is part of being teachable. Finally, there is a *corporate or national repentance.* This is when a group repents on behalf of their nation or their ancestors. For example, "Lord, we as a nation confess the sin of lying to and mistreating the Native Indians," or "Father, forgive us for the way our forefathers enslaved the Blacks."

Prayer of Repentance

Father, I thank You for the gift of repentance. I pray that You would reveal any sins in my life and bring the hidden things to light. Pour out conviction upon me. Reveal truth to me. Let me see it the way you see it. I know my thoughts are not Your thoughts. Purify my thought life. Let me see more clearly the light of Jesus. Renew my mind.

As God brings things to your mind, confess them as sin and determine to make them right and to stop doing the sin.

We have often been reminded that Christianity is not a set of rules but a relationship with God. Let me add a kingdom component to that revelation. Christianity is not a set of rules but a relationship with the Ruler.

Repentance begins with a change of mind that leads to a change of heart and a change of lifestyle. Repentance turns us away from sins and turns us toward faith in God. The change of heart could be called conversion. Conversion means to do a u-turn. Conversion is the visible portion of repentance coupled with believing.

Faith

Faith toward God is the second part of seeing the government of God. Faith is absolutely necessary "But without faith it is impossible to please Him: for he who comes to God must believe that He is" (Heb. 11:6 KJV). Faith is the most vital step in coming into the kingdom, for without it you would not take the other steps. Faith functions at every step. We have often made it the only step, but it is significant that Peter stood on the Day of Pentecost and told the crowd to repent, and be baptized, and receive the Holy Spirit. Faith was not emphasized, in fact, it was not even mentioned.

Believing in Jesus as LORD is where faith starts (see Rom. 10:9-13). Too often we point to a Savior instead of pointing to our Lord. The gospel of the kingdom points to the King. Faith without works is dead, or in other words faith that Jesus is Lord without subsequent action, obeying that Lord, is not really faith. In Acts 6:7 (NIV) it says, "So the word of God spread. The number of disciples in Jerusalem increased rapidly, and a large number of priests *became obedient to the faith*." Faith is more than a mental concept. It is the springboard to obedience.

In Romans 10:10, we are told "with the mouth confession is made unto salvation." Faith must be verbally expressed as well as acted on. In John 3:16 we are told that whoever believes in Him, the Son, will not perish. The Greek verb for believe is in the continuous tense. So it is really saying whoever continues to believe in Him will not perish. Faith is continual.

Throughout the New Testament we are told to believe in the Lord Jesus. Not once in the context of seeing and entering the kingdom, becoming a disciple, are we told to receive Jesus into our hearts. Jesus is a human. "For there is...one Mediator...the *Man* [anthropos] *Christ Jesus*" (1 Tim. 2:5 NIV). He is in Heaven interceding for us. He occasionally visits the planet. Because He is a human, He cannot live in our hearts, except by His Spirit. We are told to receive His Spirit (see Act 2:38). We *believe* in the Lord Jesus and *receive* the Holy Spirit. Teaching someone to receive Jesus into their heart only confuses things.

When we teach new converts to ask Jesus into their hearts we do them a disservice. Yes, I know many people became Christians that way. Maybe it was the only way available at the time. When we used that method of conversion—asking Jesus into our hearts—we were only following traditions passed on to us. You cannot find an example anywhere in the whole New Testament where in the process of becoming a Christian someone was told to ask Jesus into their heart. We are expressly told in the Word to believe that Jesus is Lord and to receive the Holy Spirit. "But as many as received Him, to them He gave the right to become children of God, to those who believe in His name" (John 1:12). This is the only verse that mentions receiving Jesus and it is not into our hearts but means recognizing who He is. The verse even clarifies the issue by mentioning to those who believe.

There is so much wrong with the concept of "asking Jesus into our heart," it is hard to know where to begin. The concept is based on a wrong understanding of what the heart is and where it is. So begins the confusion. Remember, the heart is the subconscious mind. The heart is one place where God writes His law. The spirit of a man resides in his belly. That is why so many of us preachers end up with a large belly—because we are so full of spirit. Jesus said out of your belly would flow rivers of living water by which He was referring to the Holy Spirit.

*He that believeth on Me, as the scripture hath said, out of his belly shall flow rivers of living water. (But this spake He of the Spirit, which they that **believe** on Him should **receive**: for the Holy Ghost was not yet given; because that Jesus was not yet glorified)* (John 7:38-39 KJV).

It is likely that when the Spirit comes to reside within us that He resides in the belly or gut. Do you ever get a gut felling about something?

As I have mentioned, Jesus is a Man. He cannot physically occupy your heart. It would be like the biggest tumor ever known. It doesn't matter if the heart you are thinking of is the blood pump, the seat of emotions, the subconscious mind, or the belly. It would kill you to have a Man there. So it is then reasoned that when we ask Jesus to come live in our hearts that He sends His Spirit into our hearts in answer to that prayer. So then it is really the same as receiving the Spirit.

There are two problems with that. First of all, it has no substance or basis in Scripture. Second, it does not look the same in its fulfillment. I have seen that people who properly receive the Holy Spirit speak in tongues or prophesy. People who ask Jesus into their hearts do not manifest the same reaction.

It is time to quit defending our traditions and discard them in light of clear, sound biblical truth. Asking Jesus into our hearts may have been used by leading evangelists and in many churches, but that does not validate it or make it true. It is only an introduction to Jesus, not a step of discipleship. It is only a short cut to conversion, which is why in evangelical circles many converts fall away.

This reminds me of the time we had a visiting speaker from England in our church teach about team leadership. Team leadership was the newest and latest thing and would do wonders for our church. We were told to have core leaders and support leaders, so we formed two teams—the core leadership team and the support team. It was great in that in got a lot of people involved and life was sweet until a problem arose. A problem came along, and we searched the Word for a solution.

The problem was exacerbated by the fact that we could not fix it with Scripture because Scripture refers to deacons and elders, not team members. I am not against innovation and involvement; but I have found that if one uses biblical constructs, then when something goes wrong there is biblical advice to correspond to it. Long story short, we now have plurality of elders, we use Bible definitions for elders, and it seems to be functioning fine. (Amen!) What I am saying is we do ourselves a disservice when we stray away from the clear teaching of the Word and substitute different definitions or practices or short cuts for what the Bible says.

This is illustrated by the word baptism. Baptism is an Anglicized word from the Greek word *bapto,* to dip or immerse. Since the practice in the church was to sprinkle the translators from the Latin into the vernacular—common tongue, in this case English—they decided it best to invent a new word, baptize, rather than use the clear translation, dip. Greek police officers regularly baptize their donuts into their coffee. The translators did not feel free to translate *bapto* accurately because it would have contradicted religious practice. Therefore, I believe that the traditions of men nullified the Word of God.

Faith is the most important step of the four steps of the new birth. Its focus is the Lord Jesus. Faith is seen by actions of obedience. Faith is not a one-time confession but an ongoing continual trusting in the Lord. Faith toward God includes both trust and obedience. Faith without appropriate action is useless. The appropriate action when dealing with Almighty God is to do exactly what He says and trust that He is right.

Chapter Ten

Baptisms

Water Baptism

Water baptism and baptism with the Holy Spirit together constitute the steps of *entering* the kingdom. By repentance and faith, we see the lordship of Jesus and now we *obey* that lordship by doing what He commanded. Jesus commissioned us to make disciples by baptizing them. Baptism is a vital step in becoming a disciple.

> *He who believes and is baptized will be saved; but he who does not believe will be condemned* (Mark 16:16).

The two steps involved in entering the kingdom are much more controversial in the religious world than the two steps of seeing—repentance and faith. It is almost as if baptism was targeted by the enemy and purposely brought into confusion, corruption, and controversy. It would seem the adversary understands the importance of baptism better than many of the saints.

I once spoke in a friend's church on the subject of baptism. I knew that it was potentially controversial, so I offered to let him scrutinize my notes prior to the meeting. I am happy to submit to local leadership when I can. He declined the offer. So I shared in the meeting that day biblical insights on water baptism. The church was a community evangelical church made up of a mixed membership who ranged from Baptist to Mennonite to Pentecostal. It was located in a small town south of Calgary in cattle country. My pastor friend initially was fine with what I taught; but after a few of the elders chatted with him, he was really upset with me.

I had stepped on some toes and upset some sacred cows. So I asked my pastor friend what he personally thought about water baptism. His reply was baptism is not a requirement but more of an option. Then he refined his answer to say it was a compulsory option. That is political double speak. And it indicates the compromises we have made over the years with tradition. I asked him, "If Paul the apostle came to a group of believers who had not been baptized, what do you think he would do?" My friend finally conceded that Paul would have taught them to be baptized and seen to it that they were.

I have heard that more saints have been martyred for restoring the truth of baptism to the church than for any other truth. In some cultures it is all right to believe, but the minute you are baptized you are cast out of the family and sometimes even killed. Many churches practice infant baptism as a christening ritual and many churches simply sprinkle water rather than immerse people into it. Some denominations prefer to wait for a while to see if the conversion is real before they baptize in water. Some places have taught to wait as long as you can, even right up until you are on your deathbed, to be baptized so that all your sins are washed away. Baptism is a topic fraught with confusion.

It's interesting to note that when Jesus commissioned His followers to make disciples, He told them to teach the new disciples to obey all that He commanded. That is completely inclusive. Among the many instructions Jesus gave, baptism was one. Jesus highlights this one command above the rest by mentioning it specially, as vital to the process of making a disciple. A disciple is someone who has left the kingdom or control of sin and entered the kingdom or rule of Christ.

Water baptism represents the transfer from one kingdom to the other. It represents dying to the old way of life and to the old support system and being raised up in a new life. Water baptism identifies us with death, burial, and resurrection.

*Or do you not know that as many of us as were **baptized** into Christ Jesus were baptized into His **death**? Therefore we were **buried** with Him through baptism into death, that just as Christ was raised from the dead by the glory of the Father, even so we also should walk in **newness of life**. For if we have been united* *together in the likeness of His death, certainly we also shall be in the likeness of His resurrection, knowing this, that our old man was **crucified** with Him, that the body of sin might be done away with, that we should **no longer be slaves of sin**. For he who has died has been freed from sin. Now if we died with Christ, we believe that we shall also live with Him, knowing that Christ, having been raised from the dead, dies no more. Death no longer has dominion over Him. For the death that He died, He died to sin once for all; but the life that He lives, He lives to God. Likewise you also, reckon yourselves to be dead indeed to sin, but alive to God in Christ Jesus our Lord* (Romans 6:3-11).

Death frees us from the control of sin. In the story of Israel's deliverance from Egypt, you will recall that they crossed the Red Sea. This is symbolic of baptism, "Moreover, brethren, I do not want you to be unaware that all our fathers were under the cloud, all passed through the sea, all were *baptized* into Moses in the cloud and *in the sea*" (1 Cor. 10:1-2) What died in the Red Sea during that great event? Pharaoh had sent his whole army after the Israelites to force them to return to slavery. His army represented the military might of Egypt. The ability of Egypt—representative of the power of sin—to force God's people back into slavery was killed that day. Sin's ability to force us back into its control is put to death in baptism.

The blood of the lamb saved the first born sons of Israel from the death angel. Baptism in the Red Sea saved Israel from being forced to return to serve Pharaoh. The water saved them from Pharaoh's, or sin's, control, "knowing this, that our old man was *crucified* with Him, that the body of sin might be done away with, that we should *no longer be slaves of sin*" (Rom. 6:6). We are no longer slaves to sin. That water saves may seem strange but read First Peter 3:20-21.

*God waited patiently in the days of Noah while the ark was being built. In it only a few people, eight in all, were **saved through water**, and this water symbolizes **baptism that now saves** you also—not the removal of dirt from the body but the pledge of a clear conscience toward God. **It saves you by the resurrection** of Jesus Christ* (1 Peter 3:20-21 NIV).

We have had it taught to us that Jesus' death saves us. This is, of course, very true, but the Word also teaches that His resurrection saves us. Remember, saved means salvaged from sin, not just safe from hell. The blood saves you from death and hell. The resurrection saves you from having to live according to the world's system of government. We are cut off from the flesh.

Crucifixion is the ultimate circumcision or cutting off of the flesh, "knowing this, that our old man was *crucified* with Him, that the body of sin might be done away with" (Rom. 6:6). The whole body of sin is killed in crucifixion. The *sign* of the old covenant was circumcision. In circumcision, a part of the flesh was cut off. In the new covenant, circumcision is more complete. It is a circumcision of the heart and involves the cutting off of all flesh. The flesh must be cut off, killed, and buried. The sign of the old covenant was a physical act. The new covenant requires a physical act as well. This physical act of immersion in water carries power and spiritual impact.

> *For in Christ all the fullness of the Deity lives in bodily form, and you have been given fullness in Christ, who is the head over every power and authority.* ***In Him you were also circumcised, in the putting off of the sinful nature,*** *not with a circumcision done by the hands of men but with the circumcision done by Christ,* ***having been buried with Him in baptism*** *and raised with Him through your faith in the power of God, who raised Him from the dead* (Colossians 2:9-12 NIV 1984).

In the story of Israel's deliverance from Egypt and the story of Noah, water was involved in the transfer or deliverance of God's people from one world into the next. Israel came out of Egypt and into the wilderness and ultimately the Promised Land. Noah and his family were lifted out of a dying world and later deposited onto a new world. Water baptism is involved in our transfer from one kingdom to another.

> *He has delivered us from the power of darkness and* ***conveyed*** *us into the kingdom of the Son of His love* (Colossians 1:13).

Water baptism in a kingdom context has to do with *entering* the kingdom of God. It is the first outward sign of obedience or the evidence of faith. Because faith must be a component and because entering the kingdom is an act of free will, I believe that infant baptism cannot be valid. The infant is not making an informed choice. It is not his or her faith that is prompting obedience. Without faith on the part of the participant, baptism is useless. Water baptism itself cannot save. God has no grandchildren. Every child of God must choose for him or herself to serve God.

We are saved by faith, but faith without obedience is useless. In baptism, by faith, we identify with the death, burial, and resurrection of Christ. By faith, we are conveyed from the kingdom of darkness into the kingdom of light. By faith, we die to sin and are buried by immersion in water and we emerge from the water in newness of life symbolizing the resurrection. How do we *know that our old self was crucified with Him?* We know by faith.

Questions you might have: Does immersion in water convey us from one kingdom to the other or is it just symbolic of it? Is it an actual circumcision or just symbolic? Is it an actual crucifixion and burial or just symbolic? Personally, I think there is actually more going on than we have realized.

I believe that immersion in water is a physical act with spiritual consequences. I believe water baptism cuts us off from sin's ability to force us back into serving it. You can still choose to serve sin if you want to, but it cannot force you back into slavery. I believe that the reason Jesus mentioned baptism when He told His followers to make disciples (see Matt. 28:18-20) was because it represents better than any other picture, death to the old way of life and a new beginning.

Please read Romans 6:3-11 a couple more times.

> *Or do you not know that as many of us as were* **baptized** *into Christ Jesus were baptized into His* **death***? Therefore we were* **buried** *with Him through baptism into death, that just as Christ was raised from the dead by the glory of the Father, even so we also should walk in* **newness of life***. For if we have been united together in the likeness of His death, certainly we also shall be in the likeness of His resurrection, knowing this, that our old man was* **crucified** *with Him, that the body of sin might be done away with, that we should* **no longer be slaves of sin***. For he who has died has been freed from sin. Now if we died with Christ, we believe that we shall*

*also live with Him, knowing that Christ, having been raised from the dead, dies no more. Death no longer has dominion over Him. For the death that He died, He died to sin once for all; but the life that He lives, He lives to God. **Likewise you also, reckon yourselves to be dead indeed to sin, but alive to God in Christ Jesus our Lord.***

Baptism is a Greek word meaning dip. Immersion is a proper English equivalent. Since we are buried in baptism and since buried means covered over, sprinkling with water just doesn't make the grade. Immersion was a practice of the church in the years following Christ's return to Heaven. Later it was replaced by sprinkling in some denominations.

In Acts 18:8 under the ministry of Paul, "Crispus, the synagogue ruler, and his entire household believed in the Lord; and many of the Corinthians who heard him believed and were baptized" (NIV). It was very common to receive the Holy Spirit immediately after immersion although some receive the Spirit before immersion in water (see Acts 10:44-47).

*While Apollos was at Corinth, Paul took the road through the interior and arrived at Ephesus. There he found some disciples and asked them, "Did you receive the Holy Spirit when you believed?" They answered, "No, we have not even heard that there is a Holy Spirit." So Paul asked, "Then what baptism did you receive?" "John's baptism," they replied. Paul said, "John's baptism was a baptism of repentance. He told the people to believe in the One coming after him, that is, in Jesus." On hearing this **they where baptized into the name of the Lord Jesus.** When Paul placed his hands on them, the Holy Spirit came on them, and they spoke in tongues and prophesied* (Acts 19:1-6 NIV).

This initial experience of receiving the Holy Spirit and speaking in tongues is referred to by many as the baptism of the Holy Spirit. In the first century, it was considered an essential component of the life of the believer. In one situation, in Acts 10:44, the gift of the Holy Spirit was poured out on Gentiles before they had been water baptized. This astonished the Jewish believers for they heard these

Gentiles speaking in tongues and praising God. Peter immediately ordered these new believers to be immersed in water.

Please note the following from the Acts 19 passage. Even though the disciples or believers had previously been baptized, they had to be baptized again properly. Even if you were baptized as a baby you need to be baptized properly. So here is a precedent. While normally we say there is only one baptism and it need not be repeated, if the first experience was invalid, then it must be done again properly.

Also note that although Jesus commanded that believers be immersed—baptized—into the name of the Father, the Son, and the Holy Spirit, the disciples baptized people into the *name of the Lord Jesus Christ.* The word Father is not a name. Our heavenly Father has a proper name. The word son is not a name. The son has a name and so does the Spirit. Jesus is the Greek name of the Son. Jesus or Yeshua means Savior. The name of the Father is LORD in English or Yahweh in Hebrew, "I am the LORD; that is My name" (Isa. 42:8 NIV). The Holy Spirit is symbolized by oil, the anointing. The word *Christos* means the anointing or the anointed one, "God has made this Jesus, whom you crucified, both Lord and Christ" (Acts 2:36 NIV 1984). So put it all together: the name of the Father *LORD,* the name of the Son *Jesus* and the name of the Spirit *Christ.* We are baptized into the name of the LORD Jesus Christ in whom dwells the fullness of the God-head—the Father, the Son and the Holy Spirit (see Col. 2:9).

Please also note that in all the references to water baptism in the Scripture, the prerequisite was that they had repented and believed in Jesus. It is a believer's baptism because, of course, it is a step of obedience to a new faith in Christ. Baptism is invalid if the initiate, person being baptized, is not a follower of Jesus Christ. Babies are incapable of making such a decision.

Immersion in water is a vital step in the process of coming under new management. In the water, the power of sin to control you is broken or severed from you. It is a physical act with spiritual consequences. It is the circumcision of all the flesh—the crucifixion of the old self. In the water, we die to our old life; and as we come out of the water, we start life afresh. It is so powerful that the adversary has done everything he can to obscure its importance or obliterate its significance.

Baptism in the Holy Spirit

The fourth step of initiation or new birth into the government of God or rule of Christ is to be filled with the Holy Spirit. In our comparison to natural birth, this is analogous to breathing. The Greek word *pneuma* means breath or spirit. Breathing is, of course, essential to life. The Holy Spirit is given to us to empower us to prosper in the kingdom of God. The Holy Spirit is essential to spiritual life.

> *There is therefore now no condemnation to those who are in Christ Jesus, who do not walk according to the flesh, but according to the Spirit. For the law of the Spirit of life in Christ Jesus has made me free from the law of sin and death. For what the law could not do in that it was weak through the flesh, God did by sending His own Son in the likeness of sinful flesh, on account of sin: He condemned sin in the flesh,* **that the righteous requirement of the law might be fulfilled in us** *who do not walk according to the flesh but according to the Spirit. For those who live according to the flesh set their minds on the things of the flesh, but those who live according to the Spirit, the things of the Spirit. For to be carnally minded is death, but to be spiritually minded is life and peace. Because the carnal mind is enmity against God; for it is not subject to the law of God, nor indeed can be. So then, those who are in the flesh cannot please God. But you are not in the flesh but in the Spirit, if indeed the Spirit of God dwells in you. Now if anyone does not have the Spirit of Christ, he is not His. And if Christ is in you, the body is dead because of sin, but the Spirit is life because of righteousness. But if the Spirit of Him who raised Jesus from the dead dwells in you, He who raised Christ from the dead will also give life to your mortal bodies through His Spirit who dwells in you* (Romans 8:1-11).

The Holy Spirit is more than life to us, He is Lord. He is the Administrator of God's kingdom on earth. When God designed the new covenant, He decided to write the law into our hearts and minds. The law—Ten Commandments—was given on the day of Pentecost at Mount Sinai 50 days after the Passover, which activated Israel's release from Egypt. That law was in effect, God's government. In the new covenant, on the day of Pentecost, the Spirit was given. He is God's government. The kingdom of God is the rule of Christ, the Holy Spirit.

Modern teaching that is antinomian in nature—all grace and no law—has failed to convey the vital importance of Romans 8:4, "the righteous requirements of the law might be fully met in us." The example of Israel more than adequately conveys humankind's total inability to obey God's laws. We admit that we ourselves cannot fully meet all the righteous requirements of the law. The truth is, we cannot, but the Holy Spirit in us can.

God found something wrong with the first covenant. He found fault with the people. There was nothing wrong with the law He authored. It was man's inability to comply with that good law that led God to design a new covenant. As you read about this in Hebrews chapter 8, note that with the new covenant He takes the law, the same law, that was external and internalizes it by writing it on two new tablets our minds and our hearts. His purpose is clear. He wants us to know Him as Lord. Lord is who He is.

*For if that first covenant had been faultless, then no place would have been sought for a second. Because **finding fault with them** [the people], He says: "Behold, the days are coming, says the Lord, when I will make a new covenant with the house of Israel and with the house of Judah—not according to the covenant that I made with their fathers in the day when I took them by the hand to lead them out of the land of Egypt; because they did not continue [remain faithful] in My covenant, and I disregarded them, says the Lord. For this is the covenant that I will make with the house of Israel after those days, says the Lord: **I will put My laws in their mind and write them on their hearts;** and I will be their God, and they shall be My people. None of them shall teach his neighbor, and none his brother, saying, **'Know the Lord,'** for all shall know Me, from the least of them to the greatest of them. For I will be merciful to their unrighteousness, and their sins and their lawless deeds I will remember no* *more." In that He says, "A new covenant," He has made the first obsolete. Now what is becoming obsolete and growing old is ready to vanish away* (Hebrews 8:7-13).

*A new heart also will I give you, and a new spirit will I put within you: and I will take away the stony heart out of your flesh, and I will give you an heart of flesh. And **I will put My spirit within you, and cause you to walk in My statutes, and** ye shall keep My judgments, and do them. And ye shall dwell in the land that I gave to your fathers; **and ye shall be My people, and I will be your God*** (Ezekiel 36:26-28 KJV).

The New International Version says, "I will put My Spirit in you and move you to follow My decrees and be careful to keep My laws." God desires obedient children. He puts His Spirit into us to empower us to keep His laws. Paul's letter to the Romans says it this way, "the mind controlled by the Spirit is life and peace." Yes, as bad as it may sound, God is into mind control. Stop and think about it. Either sin and the flesh control your thinking—or God does. Take your pick. Jesus chose to let the Spirit control His thinking. God wants to reprogram our thinking so that we can live and act like Jesus. He gives us files to download into our hard drive—He writes His laws in our minds and hearts. Then He sends the Holy Spirit who gives us power to run those programs.

I hope that this speaks to you. The gift of the Holy Spirit is to empower us to do the will of God as expressed in His Word. The Holy Spirit is grace to us. The Holy Spirit is what makes this new covenant the covenant of grace. When the Bible says we are under grace, it means we are under the management of the Holy Spirit. Grace sits on a throne. Grace comes and fixes what was missing in the old covenant. It doesn't fix the law of God, it fixes us. There is no possible way to live in the kingdom of God without the Holy Spirit. There is no possible way of becoming a *huios* without the indwelling power of the Holy Spirit.

Is it possible to receive the Holy Spirit without being baptized in the Holy Spirit? That is an interesting question. By why would you ask that question? I had mentioned that I taught on the baptism of the Holy Spirit at a seminary in Ternopil, Ukraine. There was a young man whose father was a Baptist pastor. He said that he didn't believe the same thing about the baptism of the Holy Spirit as I did until after he heard my teaching, and then he did. There is definitely teaching out there that makes it seem that the infilling of the Holy Spirit is automatic at conversion. So there is controversy and there is confusion, hence the question.

But why live with an unanswered question? Why not live with a certainty. How do you know that you belong to God? How do you know that you are in the kingdom? "The Spirit Himself bears witness with our spirit that we are children of God" (Rom. 8:16). The Holy Spirit is our seal or guarantee that we are in the kingdom. So we'd better be certain.

> *In Him you also trusted, after you heard the word of truth, the gospel of your salvation; in whom also, having believed, you were sealed with the Holy Spirit of promise, who is the **guarantee** of our inheritance until the redemption of the purchased possession, to the praise of His glory* (Ephesians 1:13-14).

Knowing that we have the promised Holy Spirit is vital to our own confidence. The point I want to make is that we shouldn't be wondering to what degree we are filled or not filled or whether or not we have been baptized. We can know and we should know. How? By the Word of God.

First of all there are different expressions or levels of the Spirit. The Spirit can be on you or in you. You can be filled with the Spirit, led of the Spirit, and full of power as was Jesus in Luke chapter 4. These are not all synonymous but represent different levels.

> *Then Jesus, being **filled with the Holy Spirit**, returned from the Jordan and was **led by the Spirit** into the wilderness, being tempted for forty days by the devil. And in those days He ate nothing, and afterward, when they had ended, He was hungry. Now when the devil had ended every temptation, he departed from Him until an opportune time. Then Jesus returned **in the power of the Spirit** to Galilee, and news of Him went out through all the surrounding region* (Luke 4:1-2, 13-14).

The thing is, we can be filled with the Spirit but we leak. Ephesians 5:18 tells us to be filled with the Spirit; and the way it is worded in the Greek language conveys the meaning of be **continually** filled with the Spirit. The Holy Spirit was working on you even before you accepted the Lord, "No one can say that Jesus is Lord except by the Holy Spirit" (1 Cor. 12:3). So we know that every born-again believer has had at least some encounter to some degree with the Holy Spirit. We are not all led of the Spirit. We are not all full of power like Jesus was after being tempted. But we have all had some exposure. The amount of exposure may be hard to quantify, but the nice thing is that the *baptism of the Holy Spirit* can be definitively quantified.

Let's see what the Word says about what happened in the early church.

> *I baptize you with water, but He will* **baptize** *[immerse] you with the Holy Spirit* (Mark 1:8 NIV).

We have the promise of something definite by the prophet John.

> *On one occasion, while he was eating with them, he gave them this command: "Do not leave Jerusalem, but wait for the gift my Father promised, which you have heard me speak about. For John baptized with water, but in a few days you will* **be baptized** *[immersed] with the Holy Spirit"* (Acts 1:4-5 NIV).

We have the affirmation by Jesus that the Spirit will come soon.

> *When the day of Pentecost came, they were all together in one place. Suddenly the sound like the blowing of a violent wind came from heaven and filled the whole house where they were sitting. They saw what seemed to be tongues of fire that separated and came to rest on each of them. All of them were* **filled** *with the Holy Spirit and began to* **speak in other tongues** *as the Spirit enabled them* (Acts 2:1-4 NIV).

The promised Holy Spirit baptism comes. It was on the day of Pentecost, which celebrated when God first gave them His law. They spoke with tongues. Peter stands up and preaches to the crowd that what they are witnessing is the fulfillment of biblical promise by the prophet Joel. There was no wondering on the part of the disciples.

They knew that they had the baptism Jesus spoke of. People were invited to participate in the outpouring by first repenting.

In the last days, God says, I will pour out My Spirit on all people... (Acts 2:17 NIV).

Peter replied, "Repent and be baptized, every one of you, in the name of Jesus Christ for the forgiveness of your sins. And you will receive the gift of the Holy Spirit" (Acts 2:38 NIV).

The message now goes to the Samaritans, and Philip preaches to them. They believe and are baptized. Later the apostles come and lay hands on them to receive the Holy Spirit. Simon sees that with the laying on of hands, the Holy Spirit is imparted. Simon, who has witnessed miracles and healings done by Philip, is so impressed by the visible manifestation of the Spirit that he offers the apostles money.

But there was a certain man called Simon, who previously practised sorcery in the city and astonished the people of Samaria, claiming that he was someone great, to whom they all gave heed, from the least to the greatest, saying, "This man is the great power of God." And they heeded him because he had astonished them with his sorceries for a long time. But when they believed Philip as he preached the things concerning the kingdom of God and the name of Jesus Christ, both men and women were baptized. Then Simon himself also believed; and when he was baptized he continued with Philip, and was amazed, seeing the miracles and signs which were done. Now when the apostles who were at Jerusalem heard that Samaria had received the word of God, they sent Peter and John to them, who, when they had come down, prayed for them that they might receive the Holy Spirit. For as yet He had fallen upon none of them. They had only been baptized in the name of the Lord Jesus. Then they laid hands on them, and they received the Holy Spirit. And when Simon saw that through the laying on of the apostles' hands the Holy Spirit was given, he offered them money, saying, "Give me this power also, that anyone on whom I lay hands may receive the Holy Spirit." But Peter said to him, "Your money perish with you, because you thought that the gift of God could be purchased with money! You have neither part nor portion in this matter, for your *heart is not right in the sight of God. **Repent** therefore of this your wickedness, and pray God if perhaps the thought of your heart may be forgiven you. For I see that you are poisoned by bitterness and bound by iniquity."Then Simon answered and said, "Pray to the Lord for me, that none of the things which you have spoken may come upon me"* (Acts 8:9-24).

Read Acts 8:9-24 a few times. There is some powerful information there. First of all, we see all four elements of the new birth. Repentance, faith, water baptism, and the baptism of the Holy Spirit are all present. You will notice that after the people had believed and were baptized, it says right there in Scripture that *the Holy Spirit had not fallen on them yet.* So that answers the question of whether or not you get the Holy Spirit automatically when you believe in Christ. You don't. And further more, they *knew* that the invisible Holy Spirit had not filled them yet. How did they know that? They knew because they did not see a visible manifestation like speaking in tongues.

Simon was amazed at what he saw Philip do. He followed Philip for a time observing miracles and signs. There is no record of him trying to bribe Philip for the power to do signs and wonders. Then the apostles come and something really must have impressed old Simon because he gets out his wallet and tries to buy the power to baptize people in the Holy Spirit. It is unlikely Simon would have offered to pay for something undetectable. He saw something. He literally saw something. There was definitely a manifestation of the Spirit.

Then the apostle Peter soundly rebuked Simon and led him in remedial repentance after using the gift of the Spirit to see that he was bound by bitterness and such. Philip had, it would seem, only really developed two steps of the four-step process. He had led the people into step 2 and step 3—belief in the Lord and immersion in water. The apostles in Jerusalem had heard that Samaria had received the Word of God and they sent Peter and John.

Peter and John, on seeing that there was a new church emerging that practiced only faith and immersion, decided to call it a new denomination—the First Church of the Believing Baptists. Not likely! What did they do? They made sure that all the steps were completed. The order of steps is not as important as the completion of all the steps. They laid hands on them to receive the Holy Spirit. Next we have the conversion of Saul.

> *Then Ananias went to the house and entered it. Placing his hands on Saul, he said, "Brother Saul, the LORD—Jesus, who appeared to you on the road as you were coming here—has sent me so that you may see again and **be filled** with the Holy Spirit"* (Acts 9:17 NIV).

Paul states in First Corinthians 14:18 that he speaks in tongues. It is likely he was baptized in the Spirit the same way the others had been so far. Then the gospel goes to the Gentiles.

> *While Peter was still speaking these words, the Holy Spirit came on all who heard the message. The circumcised believers who had come with Peter were astonished that the gift if the Holy Spirit had been **poured out** even on the Gentiles. For they heard them* ***speaking in tongues*** *and praising God* (Acts 10:44-46 NIV).

Cornelius and his house heard the gospel. They are filled with the Spirit and speak in tongues. Then Peter stands up and says we have witnessed the birth today of a new denomination—the First Church of the Believing Charismatics. Not likely! He says, "'Can anyone forbid water, that these should not be baptized who have received the Holy Spirit *just as we have?*' And he *commanded* them to be baptized in the name of the Lord" (Acts 10:47-48).

So much for baptism or immersion in water being an option. He commanded they be baptized in water. He said the Gentiles received the Holy Spirit the same way the Jews did. The same way included speaking with tongues.

So to recap the Jews, the Samaritans, and now the Gentiles all had a substantial and visible experience called the baptism in the Holy Spirit. Next we go to Ephesus. My wife and I have been to Ephesus, in Turkey, or what was once known as Ephesus. It was a great Roman city that was destroyed by a powerful enemy—the mosquito.

> *While Apollos was at Corinth, Paul took the road through the interior and arrived at Ephesus. There he found some disciples and asked them, "Did you receive the Holy Spirit when you believed?" They answered, "No, **we have not even heard that there is a***

Holy Spirit." So Paul asked, "Then what baptism did you receive?""John's Baptism," they replied. Paul said, "John's baptism was a baptism of repentance. He told the people to believe in the One coming after him, that is, in Jesus."On hearing this they where baptized into the name of the Lord Jesus. When Paul placed his hands on them, the Holy Spirit came on them, and they spoke in tongues and prophesied* (Acts 19:1-6 NIV).

This passage is straight forward. When these believers received the Holy Spirit, they spoke in tongues and prophesied. Again, just like on the day of Pentecost. Now to get the most of this passage, we must acquaint ourselves with the previous chapter. Apollos came to Ephesus and preached what he knew. He had only the baptism of John. He spoke accurately, the Word says, but only of what he knew, but there were some things he didn't know. So as fervent as he was, he was not complete; and therefore, his disciples were equally lacking.

Paul notices this. He doesn't tell them they aren't disciples. They were disciples. He doesn't start a new denomination. He completes their knowledge and experience to conform with what was standard in the kingdom. "What baptism did you receive?" Paul asked. "John's baptism" was the reply. John the Baptist had made a serious impact, and this was one of the ripples that moved throughout the known world. John had told people about the One who would baptize them in the Holy Spirit, "He will baptize you with the Holy Spirit and fire" (Matt. 3:11). So his converts *had heard* about the Spirit. What they hadn't heard was that the Spirit had come on the day of Pentecost. The news of Pentecost hadn't reached them yet.

So when the text says *we have not even heard that there is a Holy Spirit*, it is poorly rendered. The word *come* is implied. It should read *we have not yet heard that the Holy Spirit is come*. Check it out if you don't want to take my word for it, but I have it on scholarly authority that the word come should be there. It makes more sense since all followers of John would have heard of the person of the Holy Spirit. So Paul is not content with their baptism of repentance and insists that they are properly immersed in the name of the Lord Jesus Christ—after which they received the baptism of the Holy Spirit and spoke in tongues.

This completes our survey of all the conversions in the Book of Acts. All of them agree and all point to a visible manifestation accompanying the baptism of the Holy Spirit, and in most cases mention tongues.

Why some people are adamantly opposed to speaking in tongues, I don't know. They need to read Glenn Arekion's book *The Power of Praying in Tongues*. I have found tongues to be blessing from God. I think it best to touch briefly on the subject of tongues even though I really want to focus on the kingdom.

Tongues

There are situations where people have prayed to receive the Holy Spirit and not spoken in tongues. In some cases, it is in a context where people are not informed of this possibility. In other cases, the people have fear because they have been taught against speaking in tongues or they have wrong concepts of what will happen. Often the reason people don't initially speak in tongues is due to them not knowing that they must talk in order for the Spirit to speak. They must move their lips, make sounds, breathe past the vocal cords. Tongues are a gift from the Holy Spirit. If you ask in faith for the Holy Spirit, expect to speak in tongues; but if you don't speak in tongues immediately, don't assume that God failed to give you the Holy Spirit. If you don't speak in tongues, we won't love you any less and neither will God.

The purpose of being filled with the Holy Spirit doesn't start or end with speaking in tongues. It does not center on tongues either. Our fellowship is centered on Christ. If you speak in tongues, don't neglect the gift God has given you, but don't just stay camped around tongues either. Once filled with the Spirit, branch out in the gifts of the Spirit (see 1 Cor. 12) like the word of knowledge or healing. Moving in the gifts is a very good thing to do.

Evidence that the Holy Spirit moves in our lives can be seen by the ministry of gifts, for example prophecy or tongues. Gifts should be used to build up others and to reach people for Christ. They should not be used as a measure for determining the level of maturity or the depth of understanding in a Christian's life. Evidence of a deep work of the Spirit is shown by how much we allow God's love to shine. The Spirit is love. The Spirit speaks of Jesus. The Spirit gives us boldness to speak of Jesus as well. The Spirit is the Spirit of truth. Spirit-filled people will respond to truth and walk in truth and speak the truth.

In the past, we have witnessed immature and zealous Christians blow the importance of speaking in tongues out of proportion. Others have spoken out against tongues. We have seen people who don't speak in tongues show more love and care for others than do some who speak in tongues. Speaking in tongues does not mean that the person is better or more special than one who doesn't. Nor is speaking in tongues evil, as some have maintained. Speaking in tongues is simply one of many wonderful gifts God has made available for us. We should value what God has seen fit to supply us with. We should not overemphasize nor ignore this or any God-given gift. We should use it and all the gifts of the Holy Spirit to build the Body of Christ.

Receiving the Holy Spirit is an essential step in initiation. It must be considered that in the early days of the church people didn't have the New Testament writings for reference. They couldn't say John's Epistle says such and such. So how did they convince people that they had, in fact, *entered* the kingdom? What did they do to bring an assurance of salvation?

> *And you also were included in Christ when you heard the message of truth, the gospel of your salvation. When you believed, you were marked in Him with a seal, the promised Holy Spirit, who is a deposit **guaranteeing** our inheritance until the redemption of those who are God's possession...* (Ephesians 1:13-14 NIV).

The subjective experience of receiving the Holy Spirit and speaking in tongues was as, if not more, important to the initiates in assurance of salvation as the objective theology. The old expression "better felt than telt" may have some validity.

Evidence of Being Spirit-Filled

*...but **be filled** with the Spirit* (Ephesians 5:18).

This passage from Ephesians is a command. In the Greek language it is actually saying be being filled or be continually or constantly filled with the Spirit. We need to be filled over and over again.

While it is the opinion of the author that a manifestation of the Spirit is sufficient evidence of our initial filling of the Spirit, our on-going life in the Spirit should be evidenced by more than just speaking in tongues—although speaking in tongues is good and should be done extensively if we want to become a *huios*.

The Holy Spirit was given to us to make us witnesses. To aid in that, He gives us boldness to testify.

> *For God has not given us a spirit of fear and timidity, but of power, love, and self-discipline. So never be ashamed to tell others about our Lord* (2 Timothy 1:7-8 NLT).

God gives us His fruit so that our character is a witness. He gives us His gifts so that His power is a witness. Also, we read in Ephesians 5:17-6:5 that to be filled with the Spirit involves speaking in psalms and hymns, singing and making melody, etc. This speaks of a love for worshiping and praising the Lord. Giving thanks, or the attitude of gratitude, is also evidence of being filled with the Spirit.

Submitting in fear of Christ—wives to husbands, children to parents, and slaves to masters—speaks of the kingdom nature of being filled with the Spirit. The Holy Spirit is not rebellious; rather it produces the fruit of submissiveness in our lives. These attitudes are also evidence of being filled with the Spirit.

Since we cannot operate in the kingdom without the Holy Spirit, it follows that part of the process involved in entering that domain is to receive the Spirit. If you have not yet been baptized in the Holy Spirit, then you should ask God to do so.

> *If a son asks for bread from any father among you, will he give him a stone? Or if he asks for a fish, will he give him a serpent*

instead of a fish? Or if he asks for an egg, will he offer him a scorpion? If you then, being evil, know how to give good gifts to your children, how much more will your heavenly Father give the Holy Spirit to those who ask Him! (Luke 11:11-13)

It also might help to have Spirit-filled fellow believers pray with you or lay hands on you.

The baptism of the Holy Spirit is the fourth step of initiation into the kingdom of God. I could write a whole book about this subject; but within the confines of this book, we have looked at the experience of the new church and how they all had visible evidence of the baptism of the Spirit. We have discussed the need of the power of the indwelling Spirit to enable us to comply with what God has written in the New Covenant in both our hearts and minds.

And we have discussed the obvious truth that in order to be led of the Spirit one must be filled with the Spirit. To be led of the Spirit is the goal of becoming a *huios* so that the righteous requirement of the law might be fully meet in us who do not walk according to the flesh but according to the Spirit (see Rom. 8:4). And finally, remember the earnest expectation of all of creation is for the revealing of the *huios* of God—so do what it takes to grow up in God and go and change the world.

Chapter Eleven

Pattern for Change

*And they continued steadfastly in the apostles' doctrine and fel-
lowship, in the breaking of bread, and in **prayers** (Acts 2:42).*

We need to grow up. We need to overcome the flesh. The flesh
needs to give way to the Spirit. How will that happen? King Saul
had an opportunity to change into a different man. King Saul represents for us our fleshly nature or that part of us that needs to change
if we are to become obedient Spirit-led sons. We can relate to Saul
therefore.

*Then Samuel took a flask of oil and poured it on his head, and
kissed him and said: "Is it not because **the Lord has anointed
you commander over His inheritance?** When you have de-
parted from me today, you will find two men by Rachel's tomb
in the territory of Benjamin at Zelzah; and they will say to
you, 'The donkeys which you went to look for have been found.
And now your father has ceased caring about the donkeys and
is worrying about you, saying, "What shall I do about my
son?"' Then you shall go on forward from there and come to the
terebinth tree of Tabor. There three men going up to God at
Bethel will meet you, one carrying three young goats, another
carrying three loaves of bread, and another carrying a skin of
wine. And they will greet you and give you two loaves of bread,
which you shall receive from their hands. After that you shall
come to the hill of God where the Philistine garrison is. And it
will happen, when you have come there to the city, that you will
meet a group of prophets coming down from the high place with*

a stringed instrument, a tambourine, a flute, and a harp before them; and they will be prophesying. Then the Spirit of the Lord will come upon you, and you will prophesy with them and be turned into another man. And let it be, when these signs come to you, that you do as the occasion demands; for God is with you. You shall go down before me to Gilgal; and surely I will come down to you to offer burnt offerings and make sacrifices of peace offerings. Seven days you shall wait, till I come to you and show you what you should do (1 Samuel 10:1-8).

God has anointed us with the Holy Spirit and enabled us to share in the inheritance. We have been given authority to be kings and priests. We have been qualified. The New Testament confirms this in Colossians:

*...we...ask that you may be filled with the knowledge of His will in all wisdom and spiritual understanding; that you may walk worthy of the Lord, fully pleasing Him, being fruitful in every good work and increasing in the knowledge of God; strengthened with all might, according to His glorious power, for all patience and longsuffering with joy; giving thanks to the Father who has **qualified us to be partakers of the inheritance** of the saints in the light. He has delivered us from the power of darkness and conveyed us into the kingdom of the Son of His love, in whom we have redemption through His blood...* (Colossians 1:9-14).

Saul was directed by Samuel to go to three places: Zelzah, Tabor, and Gilgal. Zelzah means noon and represents an appointed time. Tabor means purity and represents freedom from pollution or distraction. Gilgal means hill and represents a geographic place. I believe that God wants us to set a time and find a place free of distractions where we can have a quiet time with Him. It is in these quiet times, devotion, and spending time with Him that we will be changed.

At these three locations, three events took place. These three events can represent activities that we incorporate into a devotional time.

At *Zelzah* near Rachel's tomb, Saul was to meet two men, "they will say to you, 'The donkeys which you went to look for have been found. And now your father has ceased caring about the donkeys and is worrying about you, saying, "What shall I do about my son?"'" (1 Sam. 10:2). What is very significant is that this occurs by Rachel's tomb. Rachel was the beloved wife of Jacob.

Jacob, as you may recall, had four women in his life. Two wives and their maids all gave Jacob children. Rachel was his favorite. This is where she was buried. This is where you and I must bury what we treasure most. We must die to our cherished desires and plans. We must surrender agendas and goals to the Lord. Rather than praying to God about the things we want, we should pray, "Not my will but Thy will be done today." We let what we want to do die, and consult Him about what He wants us to do today.

God has something to say to you in this quiet time, "Don't worry about the donkeys." Saul was out looking for his father's donkeys. He was out there working for his father. God, our Father, says, "I am more concerned about you than your mission. Let's spend some quality time together." In our time alone with God, as well as surrendering our favorite desires to Him, we need to listen to Him.

Donkeys can represent our busyness, our mission, our work, ministry, or even the things that we chase after when we should be chasing after God. Stop chasing the donkeys and smell the presence of God. Put those things you love into the tomb. Don't worry. God can resurrect them if He wants to. God wants to convey His special care for you—take time to listen.

At the great tree of *Tabor,* Saul was to meet three men, "they will greet you and give you two loaves of bread" (1 Sam. 10:4). Bread represents the Word of God. Saul was to accept two out of three loaves. Some Bibles have three sections: the Old Testament, the Apocrypha, and the New Testament. We accept two: Old and New Testaments. Christians need to eat both loaves, not just nibble away on the New. The Old Testament provides the only basis or foundation on which to better understand the teaching of the New. The early church had only one Bible, the Old Testament. Yet they changed the world in which they lived.

In our quiet time with God, after dying to fleshly desires and giving Him control of our daily agenda and after listening to Him, we input the Word of God into our spirits and minds. We reprogram the hard drive. *Give us this day our daily bread.* Just like our bodies want to eat food, our spirits want to eat spiritual food. Why do we consider feeding our body three or four times per day normal, but feeding our spirits once a day a chore? It is not legalism to feed our spirit once or twice a day. It is vital if we are to prosper spiritually, "Let the word of Christ dwell in you richly in all wisdom; teaching and admonishing one another in psalms and hymns and spiritual songs, singing with grace in your hearts to the Lord" (Col. 3:16).

In *Gibeah,* Saul was to meet a procession of singing, prophesying prophets, "The Spirit of the LORD will come upon you, and you will prophesy with them and be turned into another man" (1 Sam. 10:6). The most important event was that the Spirit came upon him. During our quiet time, we should ask God to fill us afresh with the Holy Spirit. We need to be filled not just once, but constantly, continually, daily.

You will note that the prophets were singing and worshiping with music. During your time alone with God, consider worshiping and praising Him using song. Make a joyful noise unto the Lord.

> *...be filled with the Spirit, speaking to one another in psalms and hymns and spiritual songs, singing and making melody in your heart to the Lord; giving thanks always for all things to God the Father in the name of our Lord Jesus Christ* (Ephesians 5:18-20).

Some suggest that you could worship first before prayer or reading the Word. The important thing is to *get filled with the Spirit.* The overflow of that is singing, rejoicing, and thanksgiving.

Samuel told Saul he would prophesy with these men immediately after being filled with the Spirit. That, of course, agrees with the Book of Acts when people were filled with the Spirit, prophesied, or spoke in tongues. There is another important application of this. The spirit of prophecy is the testimony of Jesus. Revelation 19:10 says, "I am your fellow servant, and of your brethren who have the testimony of Jesus. Worship God! For the testimony [witness] of Jesus is the spirit of prophecy." And Jesus said in Acts 1:8, "You will receive power when the Holy Spirit comes on you; and you will be My witnesses" (NIV). We need to be filled with the Spirit to witness.

We should consider that our quiet time with God is a preparation for doing what He has called us to do, which is to build the family business, to seek and save the lost, to make disciples of all nations. We need to be filled with the Spirit to receive power and to be witnesses. The Holy Spirit also provides boldness and wisdom. The gifts of the Spirit enable us to do effective evangelism, and the fruit of the Spirit enables us to walk the walk. The leadership of the Spirit guides us into all truth. The Spirit intercedes through us as we pray in the spirit.

During this quiet time with God, it is well to pray in the spirit, tongues, for a while and also pray with understanding for people who need to become disciples. Pray for wisdom. Pray for divine appointments with people you can witness to, encourage, or heal.

Saul is told that once these signs are fulfilled to do whatever his hand finds to do. Do as the occasion demands, for God is with him. This sounds like you can now do your own thing, but stop and consider this. You have died to the flesh by putting your agenda in the tomb. You have listened to the Father. You have filled your mind with the Word of God, and you have been filled afresh with the Holy Spirit. You have spent some time worshiping the Lord and praying in tongues. You have asked for divine appointments and prayed for the lost. You are focused. You are empowered. You are anointed with power to go forth and do good, healing all those who are oppressed by the devil, for God is with you. You are ready to obey Colossians 3:17, "And whatever you do in word or deed, do all in the name of the Lord Jesus…."

The Holy Spirit enables you to change into a different person—someone who looks and acts like Jesus, the prototype *Huios*.

God anointed Jesus of Nazareth with the Holy Spirit and with power, who went about doing good and healing all who were oppressed by the devil, for God was with Him (Acts 10:38).

Daily devotions won't do us much good if they don't affect what we do with our hands. In other words, after spending quality time with God building faith, go out and do practical things with your hands that show the love of God to this dying world.

Finally, Samuel instructed the new king to wait seven days for further instructions.

> *You shall go down before me to Gilgal; and surely I will come down to you to offer burnt offerings and make sacrifices of peace offerings. Seven days you shall wait, till **I come to you and show you what you should do*** (1 Samuel 10:8).

You and I need to learn how to hear from God and how to be led of the Spirit. We need to become intimate with the Father, obedient to the Lord Jesus, and filled with the Holy Spirit. This is our vital necessity. We also need to hear God speak through anointed men and women of God, especially those God has given to us as leaders, mentors, or instructors, "Obey those who rule over you, and be submissive, for they watch out for your souls" (Heb. 13:17). Jesus has given us various instructors to help us mature. We need to listen to them as well as have devotions.

> *And He Himself gave some to be apostles, some prophets, some evangelists, and some pastors and teachers, **for the equipping of the saints** for the work of ministry, for the edifying of the body of Christ, till we all come to the unity of the faith and of the knowledge of the Son of God, to a perfect man, to the measure of the stature of the fullness of Christ; that we should no longer be children...* (Ephesians 4:11-14).

This chapter was written to give you a pattern for daily devotions. Many useful patterns exist. The Lord's Prayer and the Tabernacle of Moses also serve as patterns. You can try a variety of them. You can pray the Word of God. I've given you Colossians 1:9-14 as an example. You can pray in the Spirit. The essential truth is simply this: if you want to grow up in the kingdom, you need to die to self, to the flesh, learn the Word of God, and be constantly filled with the Holy Spirit. You need to grow in faith by reprogramming your mind with the Word and by doing works of faith. Effort is required. It also helps to have fellowship and support of like-minded saints.

This concludes the section focused on kingdom of God foundations. The final chapter is about how we started Huios House. It shares our principle values and the activities we use to assist us and others to become Spirit-led. I add it for your edification and comfort.

By now you should know what a *huios* is and have a new perspective on lordship and the law. You have been introduced to the concept of obedience being expected by the Lord and how the traditions of men have tried to remove it from our faith walk by calling it legalism. We who are by nature wild have been grafted onto the root of the cultivated olive tree—the Jews—and it is important to learn about our roots by absorbing the Old Testament.

The new birth has been explained in detail; and if you are lacking any of the vital components, you should seek to complete the whole process by adding any component you lack.

The path to becoming a *huios* is full of obstacles and requires effort, but pockets of overcomers are springing up all around the globe. Embrace your destiny. Become all you can be. Build your house on the Rock—the LORD Jesus. Be filled with the Spirit. Be led of the Spirit. Be empowered by the Spirit.

Then go and change nations for His glory.

Chapter Twelve

Vision of Huios House

Huios House Church Conception and Inception
Canmore, Alberta, 2008

Envision, if you will, a new concept in fellowship that is based on the premise that all believers have been gifted and anointed by God to some degree. Picture a gathering that allows each member to function in the capacity of a minister. Imagine a group where members are valued and appreciated for participating, not just occupying a seat. Visualize a learning experience where you can be enriched by others, and they in turn are enriched by you.

Does this sound like chaos or life to you?

Imagine a meeting that anticipates the Holy Spirit to administrate. Where individuals are encouraged to grow in the life of the Spirit. Where the purpose is to become led of the Spirit. Mistakes can be made, it is true, but let them be made in an atmosphere where the Word is valued and where the saints collaborate. Mature believers can and should test prophecy. At the same time, earnest attempts by people to learn to prophesy should be cultivated.

It is time the church grew up into spiritual maturity.

Perhaps our present model of doing church—singing, announcements, sermon—can be improved upon, but that might be like sewing a patch of new cloth on an old garment. The pastor-led church can conceivably become a Spirit-led church, but only when the pastor is willing to die to human expectations. The early church was not pastor-led. The purpose of the pastor was similar to that of a parent. In our home, everyone speaks, not just the parents. The children grow up. They leave home. They start their own families. It is time for the children to grow up spiritually.

Our most common church experience is based on the following. The Jesus we worship is primarily a Savior. The central tenant of our faith is that we are saved. Grace is seen as mercy and rules are seen as legalism. Our gospel is "me" centered. Above all things we value freedom. We are expected to attend meetings, give money, and grow in Christian character. We aren't expected to heal the sick, raise the dead, multiply loaves and fishes, confront religious people, or prophesy in the marketplace. We have become a subculture that is relatively ineffective at changing society.

The early church saw Jesus primarily as LORD. They were disciples. Grace was understood to mean enablement and rules were seen as part of living under His lordship. The gospel was kingdom centered. Freedom was freedom from sin not freedom from responsibility. They changed the world.

Isn't it time you broke the bonds of human tradition and embraced your destiny? Does something stir deep inside you to reach for more of God's life? Are you tired of the same old same old? Do you want to move beyond being a *teknon* (immature child of God) to become a **huios** (mature son of God)? You need to hear and obey the Spirit of God. You need to be part of something that allows and encourages it.

A New Model

Every church does things a certain way. Their pattern or model is based on church history and tradition. The current model is an adaptation of the Roman Catholic model where the church is led by a priest. We call the priest a pastor, but he still functions in many ways as a mediator between us and God. Our meetings are very much like a classroom or lecture theater where we listen to a speaker. Even though it has been shown time and again that we retain little of what we hear, maybe six percent tops, we still persist in these patterns. The way the meeting is structured adapts us into being an audience and the speaker becomes a form of entertainment. There is little or no provision for audience feedback. The pastor assumes his flock is hearing his messages and growing.

Do we need a new model?

Currently the pastor seeks God for his message. He experiences some of the life of the Spirit as he leads Sunday morning. He is anointed and he is using his gifts to edify the Body. He is being used of God. He is having a good time. What about the rest of us? Why limit the anointing to one person? Who limits the anointing? Is it God or man? Acts 2:17 says, "I will pour out my Spirit on all flesh. Your sons and daughters...." Why not have a model that gives us all the same experience as the pastor?

Surely the most important thing we can do as a Christian is learn to be led of the Spirit. Think about it for a minute. What could be more important? It has been said that God is not looking for Spirit-filled people but Spirit-led people. Jesus was led by the Spirit into the wilderness and He returned empowered by the Spirit. Then He went about doing good, healing all who were oppressed. We need to go from having a small experience with the Holy Spirit to the place where He daily guides us and empowers us to do good.

Is your church teaching you this? Are you growing in this? Thirty-five years of being a Christian has taught me that we need to be led of the Spirit and we need opportunities to learn in a proper environment. Your pastor has the opportunity, and now you need it, too. We need a new model for meetings that encourages growth in the area of hearing and obeying the Spirit. This is vital to our development and our destiny.

A New Foundation

Every house needs a foundation. It's very difficult to change a foundation once the building is built. This is why it is difficult for existing churches to change. If we start fresh, let's address the issue of foundation and build it right. I believe that the foundation of the church is not supposed to be the saving grace of God, but the fact that *Jesus is Lord*. In order to be saved, we must confess that Jesus is Lord. Boss. Master. Head guy. In charge. The word Lord means in our language "He who must be obeyed." Grace is given to us by God so that we can obey. The problem of the old covenant was that the people didn't always obey. The beauty of the new covenant is that God has given us the power and presence of the Holy Spirit so that we can obey the terms of the covenant that He has written in our hearts and minds. We cannot do this in our own strength, so God provides His strength.

Jesus is the King of the kingdom. We belong to the kingdom. Jesus is our King. Sin does not rule us. The Spirit rules us. Something rules us whether it be the Spirit or sin. Christianity may be a relationship and not a set of rules, but it is a relationship with the Ruler. So first of all, main point, we have to adapt to the truth that believing in Jesus as Lord is not a religious rite of passage but an on-going, life-long commitment. Jesus really is Lord. We have to live like we believe it.

Jesus said that if we are to be His friends, we must do what He tells us to do. That is our God-given definition of intimacy. Love for God is this—that we obey His commands. These ideas have escaped us, but they have not escaped the Lord. He still thinks they are valid.

He has written His laws in our hearts and minds. They are the Ten Commandments not the Ten Suggestions. Obeying the laws of God is not the path to salvation. The laws of God reveal to us our need of salvation. Once saved, we are part of the family of God; and as part of the family, He expects us to obey. We cannot obey without the help of the Holy Spirit. That is why He filled us in the first place.

*So now there is no condemnation for those who belong to Christ Jesus. And because you belong to Him, the power of the life-giving Spirit has freed you from the power of sin that leads to death. The law of Moses was unable to save us because of the **weakness** of our sinful nature. So God did what the law could not do. He sent His own Son in a body like the bodies we sinners have. And in that body God declared an end to sin's control over us by giving His Son as a sacrifice for our sins. He did this **so that the just requirement of the law would be*** *fully satisfied in us, who no longer follow our sinful nature but instead follow the Spirit* (Romans 8:1-4 NLT).

And I will give you a new heart, and I will put a new spirit in you. I will take out your stony, stubborn heart and give you a tender, responsive heart. And I will put My Spirit in you **so that** *you will follow My decrees and* **be careful to obey** *My regulations* (Ezekiel 36:26-27 NLT).

Every house needs a foundation. Hopefully you can see that the foundation of the house of God is the LORD Jesus Christ. We must know the Lord as Lord and that we are servants. The only way to serve the Lord is by the power of the Holy Spirit. Our faith must be exercised in the area of hearing and obeying the Administrator of the church. It's all about Lord Jesus. It's not about us and our needs and wants. We must be fit for the Master's use, and we must be about our Father's business.

Are you ready to be a servant?

So having a foundation based on the *lordship of Jesus,* how do we structure meetings for developing *spiritual growth* in all believers? How do we meet together in a way that prepares all of us for ministry or that incorporates the idea that we are all anointed ministers of God? We need to share an opportunity similar to what the pastor of a local church has each week, which includes seeking the Lord, moving in the Spirit, sharing with and edifying others. Wouldn't it be great to have an atmosphere where the wisdom and gifts of each member are valued and have more anointing, more reciprocation, more growth, more life? To accomplish this, many saints are using the model of the house church.

The House Church

I read an article on a website that in New Zealand about 25 percent of Spirit-filled believers no longer attend church. I can't verify the numbers, but you could check out some websites and see for yourself. Apparently these believers are not backsliding. They are bored with warming a pew. Many of them were elders and deacons. They have started house churches. I propose we start house churches or home groups based on kingdom theology that allows mature saints to grow and develop more in the Spirit. Eventually, new believers will benefit from this model and will grow much faster than those of us steeped in tradition.

Huios House has no paid leaders. We will have plurality of elders. We develop in our understanding of kingdom theology and the practice of prophetic prayer. We learn to test prophecy and judge prophecy. We encourage one another to grow in the wisdom of God and in the fear of the Lord. We seek God separately and together. We seek His kingdom. We share our anointed gifts. We worship together and wait upon the Lord. We participate.

The thing that sets a mature believer apart from an immature believer is wisdom. Wisdom is skill. In our context, it would be skill at hearing and obeying God. The fear of the Lord is the beginning of wisdom. So we need to see the Lord as Lord, fear the Lord, and hear and obey the Spirit of the Lord. Then we need to impact our world with His power. Can a single log burn with fervent heat? Unlikely. We need to get the logs together to help one another accomplish this. We need to provoke and stimulate one another to action. We need to protect one another as we learn to hear and obey.

Initiating a New House Church

Not everyone may be ready for this. Not everyone who is disenchanted with the way church is wants to be Spirit-led, but there are some mature saints who either don't attend church or attend even though they get little out of it, who want to move on in God. The following is a model of how we established Huios House. The procedures serve only as a template—not a rigid formula.

First of all, we spread the idea of this new house church to all who might be interested. We assembled like-minded saints who wanted to help each other learn. We spent time clearly identifying what it is we want to do and how. Those who wanted to join did, and those who didn't, didn't.

We started with a few introduction meetings where the vision was clearly explained. People were encouraged to bring friends and guests at this time. Then we began with a series of about seven meetings that established the foundation. We discussed kingdom theology. Saints were encouraged to know what their gifts are and to make them known. We also learned how to judge prophecy and to help people prophesy with confidence. Then we began "regular" meetings. Hopefully "regular" meetings will not be all the same. We hope that by giving the Holy Spirit more latitude, we will experience more creativity and variety.

Throughout the year, there are regular meetings every Saturday evening. Some meetings are prayer times. Some will be food and fellowship times. Some worship sessions. Sometimes we may watch a video, such as Bill Johnson, as a catalyst for discussion. We have variety. We even have extra sessions when required. A couple times during the course of the year, a seven-week foundation study is available on a Tuesday or Wednesday evening for new members. We also offer outreach activities such as treasure hunting (see Kevin Dedmon's book, *The Ultimate Treasure Hunt*).

Our group is small and composed mostly of "eldership material." This way everyone can participate. Once we adjusted to the new model, we accommodate new growth by adding new groups or dividing the current group. There is no limit to our potential growth.

There are a few ways of structuring for small group growth. One is that the first group splits creating two new groups with some old and some new people. Another way is that the parent group keeps meeting, and members of that group have a second meeting with their new people. Those new people grow and start their own groups. Whatever way we decide to accommodate growth, the exciting challenge is to see how the Holy Spirit administrates this. Our purpose is not to form groups. It is to provide a place to grow up into mature sons of God. It is to value one another as we help one another accomplish this goal.

Dealing with the Spirit of Control

It is often the problem in church groups that certain people like to control and manipulate. We are hopeful that with a proper understanding of the kingdom of God, members of our house church will learn to fear God and not others. Nevertheless, some personalities tend to be more forthright than others, so we have a plurality of elders that while trying to allow the Holy Spirit to be in charge will also help prevent persons other than the Holy Spirit from controlling things.

Are there problems? Probably, but this is to be expected not only in the group but in our own hearts as well as we wrestle with surrendering our will to the Lord. We should not fear this or run from it. We must learn to deal with controllers in the same way as dealing with salespeople—learning sales resistance. We can learn to deal graciously but firmly.

People who tend to be easily influenced must learn to judge all things and hold fast to that which is good. Most of all, we need to learn to have one Lord—Jesus. A believer who likes to take charge will struggle with submission, but that is necessary to grow into a *huios* (mature servant and son of God). The struggle that may be apparent in the group may also serve to illustrate the internal struggle within all of us to come into adjustment to the reality of kingdom living. Having a framework to deal with this will help. Having the understanding that "struggling for control" will happen, can happen, and must happen if we are to make lordship real, can really help us give grace to one another.

Not all situations are control issues. Sometimes leadership is valid and useful and we should flow with it. Parents have more say in their own children's lives than they do in other people's children's lives. We acknowledge that we are all servants of God. He has the say. We aren't here to develop human leadership as much as we want to develop an understanding of following the Spirit's leadership. This is to say that leadership will be expressed from time to time, but it is not the emphasis.

Developing Meekness

Meekness is strength under control. As we learn to express what we feel, the Holy Spirit might be saying we will do it with a teachable attitude. Past experience has shown that some people prophesy with punch and confidence—and may not have heard from God—

while others share tentatively and without confidence—and may have heard from God. The confident ones in this example have not heard from God, but at the same time are not open to correction. Others in the group see the confidence of the one sharing and assume that their own misgivings about the shared word are invalid in light of their own lack of confidence. The quiet ones hold back, and in the end we miss out on the whole counsel of God.

Each and every prophecy is evaluated on the basis of its content—not on the basis of how confident or unconfident the one prophesying was. Each person recognizes that every word will be tested and it is the "utterance," not the speaker who is being questioned. It really helps for this to flow nicely for people with extreme confidence to preface their "utterance" with this sentiment, "I submit this to the rest of you. I think that God might be saying...." People without extreme confidence should also preface their "utterances" the same way. We all will, because we all see through a glass darkly. You can still deliver the word with punch and sparkle if that is your style; but before sparkling, take a moment to be humble so the word can be checked without bruising your ego.

Testing Prophecy

Prophecy occurs as we pray for one another. We seek to pray in the will of God for the person. Prophetic prayer can be extremely powerful and encouraging. For this we include word of wisdom and word of knowledge with prophecy. There are guidelines.

1. Prophetic prayer is not for correction or an opportunity to preach. It is not a venue for exposing sin. Prophetic prayer is for:

   • Edification (building others' faith).

   • Encouragement (building others' hope and courage).

   • Comfort (confirmation and affirmation).

2. Prophetic prayer is subject to being tested. When hearing a prophecy, the tests are:

a) Does it agree with the Word?

b) Does it edify, encourage, or comfort?

c) Does it witness with your spirit that God would speak this way?

d) Does the person getting the word agree with it? Does it confirm?

e) Is it specific or rather vague? Clear or confusing? Something that we can definitely know when it has happened or not?

Take the word in First Samuel 10, for example, "You will meet three men. One will be carrying three young goats, another carrying three loaves of bread and another carrying a skin of wine." Now this was a word you could understand when it was fulfilled. Compare it to some of the drivel we see today in prophetic publications, "A time is coming that will bring change. Blah, blah, blah." How do you judge that? Vague words do not carry water. They can be rejected. It's OK to give them, because after all, we are all learning and none of us may measure up to Samuel just yet—but we don't have to receive them.

3. Time is given for judging the words and for the person getting the words to comment.

4. The word given will be either:

a) accepted (the Word agrees, people witness, carries water), in which case it will be honored and feared.

b) unaccepted, in which case it won't be honored or feared, but the person giving it will still be accepted in the beloved. Remember, those He loves, He corrects. Embrace correction. I know it's hard.

c) shelved. Sometimes we don't know whether it's a true word or not. Shelved means we leave it for future confirmation. Sometimes the person receiving the word will confirm it. Sometimes it is confirmed years later.

5. Prophecy can have a source other than the Holy Spirit. It is possible for you to read the person's soul or to prophesy from your own soul. We don't have to blurt everything that pops into our minds. We can learn to discern. This is why it is best if words are tested. This is why it is best if we fear the Lord. It's all part of the learning process. With practice, we can self-judge the word before we give it. But when in doubt, share it to be tested and learn from the experience. Generally speaking, words concerning romance and marriage should be avoided. They are often soulish in source.

6. Occasionally you might get a word that is a rebuke. Hold on to it and pray about it. Consider giving it in private or consider asking permission of the one being prophesied to, to give it publicly so it can be tested. In my experience, it is possible for the Holy Spirit to bring a rebuke in a way that is so gentle and uplifting that the person feels honored to get it. Pray about it. Don't blurt it. And if you seem to be getting a lot of rebuking words for others, the problem may be with you. The law of sowing and reaping means that you will also be rebuked. It may be best to hide the word of rebuke in your heart and intercede for the intended target of the rebuke for a while.

In spite of the potential problems prophecy has, the potential for good outweighs the risk. Prophecy allows us to practice hearing the Spirit. We are not setting out to be a group of prophets. Prophecy is not our end goal. Our goal is to be Spirit-led. We aim to learn better how to hear from God by using the confirming atmosphere of other God-fearing people. Prophecy is a door to being Spirit-led. Prophecy, word of knowledge included, like the other gifts of the Spirit can be a tool in evangelism. It is clear in Acts 1:8 that the Holy Spirit is intent on witnessing. Our goal to be Spirit-led is not primarily for our own benefit, it is for the benefit of others. All of creation is waiting for the church to mature into *huios* (mature sons), like Jesus who went about doing good and healing all who were oppressed.

For the earnest expectation of the creation eagerly waits for the revealing of the sons [huios] *of God* (Romans 8:19).

It's not going to be easy to mature. But the Holy Spirit is committed to helping us. That is why we are given the ability to pray in tongues. Praying in tongues is encouraged.

> *Likewise the Spirit also helps us in our weaknesses. For we do not know what we should pray for as we ought, but the Spirit Himself makes intercession for us with groanings that cannot be uttered...according to the will of God. And we know* [because of that] *that all things work together for good...* (Romans 8:26-28).

The Need for Eldership

There are two constraints that allow us to experience the freedom of the Spirit without it exploding in our faces or becoming weird. When the constraint of a pastor-led meeting where everyone else is not allowed to contribute is lifted and we are free to add our two cents, things can get crazy. When people realize that they can participate in the meeting and even steer the meeting or manifest some weirdness in the meeting, then they will.

The Word says let everything be done decently and in order (see 1 Cor. 14:40). To the Evangelical church that means you shut up and listen to the speaker. To us it means more freedom than that. We are aiming at a Spirit-administrated order not the imposed order of decorum. Will it get messy at times? Perhaps. Is that a bad thing? Perhaps not. Did you learn to ski without falling a few times? But like the skier, we have two poles that may help us from falling too often. The first is the role of the elders.

The elders in this house church are in the center of things participating in the action. Elder is not an empty title given to older men to give them a sense of importance. The elders in this house church are pro-actively setting an example of learning to yield to the Holy Spirit. They are doing the stuff. They humble themselves and offer to be corrected as they prophesy. They set the tone of acceptance for all members. They make the rest of us feel valued. They are hospitable. They also test prophecy and correct where needed. They are present not to control so much as to stop others from controlling. That sounds as if they are spiritual bouncers, and in a sense they are. But that still gives us more freedom than quietly sitting in our pew. They are valuable constraints preventing weirdness.

When in meetings of the Toronto Airport Church type, things happen that are weird, and they are dealt with. I have seen demonic activity that was attributed to the Lord. Now when we are in the presence of God and a demon throws someone to the floor squirming and screeching, the Lord is behind it. But the screeching isn't a gift of the Spirit, it is simply an indication that deliverance is needed. Windmilling and twitching can be manifestations of the need to be free, not a gift from God. God has turned on the light and revealed the need. So elders deal with it. Like Jesus, they can tell the demon to shut up and then cast it out.

The second constraining influence that keeps weirdness in check is understanding kingdom theology. In the early days of America, a French philosopher noticed that democracy worked better there because the people had a strong faith in God. That strong faith in God's Word and obedience to God's laws acted to constrain lawlessness. It made democracy possible. We want a church that allows freedoms and allows each one a voice, but it only works if we are individually committed to obeying God. We need to make Jesus Lord in reality. This is not easy, and we mess up lots. But if we can all stand together in agreement that Jesus is Lord, and He has written His laws in our hearts and minds so that we will obey them, then we stand a very good chance of seeing freedom in the Spirit. Where the Spirit is LORD, there is liberty. We cannot allow the false freedom of lawlessness to choke out the life of God. On the other hand, too much law can be death to us.

The Pharisees took the commands of God and embellished them to such a degree that what was intended to set the Jews apart as the holy people of God became a major burden. The commandment concerning the Sabbath meant you could do no commerce on Saturday, you could not carry your load of produce to market. The Jews often carried a needle and thread with them. The Pharisees told them they could not carry the needle and thread on the Sabbath. They told the people that sandals with metal nails in the soles could not be worn on the Sabbath. The beauty of rest on the Sabbath became obliterated by numerous adjuncts and unnecessary burdens.

Jesus upheld the Sabbath's original intent by declaring that the Sabbath was made for man, not man for the Sabbath. We should want freedom from religious adjuncts while still obeying God's original intent like Jesus did.

Jesus condemned lawlessness. Jesus said to make disciples by teaching them to obey all that He commanded. Jesus upheld the law, but He rebuked the religious and the hypocrites. We are to walk the path of lordship avoiding the ditch of lawlessness, or license, on the one side and the ditch of legalism on the other.

How do we do this effectively? First of all, understanding the kingdom of God brings these things into proper focus. Keep the commands simple. Second, we should see the commands of God as something we should follow, but not something for which we hold others accountable. Now while it is true that we need to teach new disciples the commands of God, we do that most effectively by example. So what I am saying is: no finger pointing. Don't lay on others what you aren't doing yourself. That is hypocrisy. Do it first, and then lead by example like Jesus did.

By personally endeavoring to submit to the lordship of Jesus and by utilizing elders, we should be able to deal effectively with most of the weirdness that comes with freedom.

Qualifications for Eldership

Elders:

- Understand the kingdom of God and believe that Jesus is Lord.

- Are filled with the Holy Spirit according to Acts 1:8, Ephesians 5:17-21, Acts 10:44-46.

- Are wise—usually means they have been believers for a while.

- Are real in their faith, and it is evident in the way they conduct themselves at work and at home.

- Are apt to teach. They flow in the gifts.

- Are given to hospitality. See Titus 1:5-9.

- Oversee but do not lord it over (see 1 Pet. 5:1-4).

Doors into the Life of the Spirit

There are different practices that can assist us in learning to be Spirit-led. You have perhaps noticed that it is easier to hear from God during a time of worship. That is due to the fact we are focused on Him primarily. Sometimes a time of waiting on God can also be effective. When we meet together, opportunity will be there for those called to lead worship and/or to play instruments to use their gifts to bless God and others. We are committed to building an atmosphere that allows God to manifest Himself in power in our midst.

There are three other practices that I personally find helpful for me hear from God. At least they are things that I can experiment with and learn from.

The first of the three is the idea of praying during the week to the Lord, asking what it is He will be speaking about at the next meeting. I record any impressions and test them at the next meeting to see if God speaks through the main speaker or the prophetic word, coming from others not me, or sharing of others on that subject. If He does, you know you've heard from God and the message will be even more real to you. Don't expect to get the whole message first time. Be encouraged; this simple practice works.

Another way to hear from the Lord is to prophesy. Participating in prophecy in meetings definitely helps.

A third and very important way to learn God's leading is to pray about where your tithes and offerings should go each week. In most churches, this practice is overshadowed by the practice of simple giving each week to that local church. While this might benefit the local church, it doesn't really help you learn to give as God directs at personal level. I have been richly rewarded in times when I prayed about giving and heard what I thought was God. As an example, I once gave to an individual and got feedback that it was exactly what the person needed to the penny. It's very good to feel you've done the right thing.

Another personal example concerned giving a large gift which would require us to make sacrifices. We received a check in the mail a week later for ten times the amount we gave. God is good.

I understand that when you attend a local church you feel it is right to support it financially. Dare I ask, has this faithful diligence led to you walking in the Spirit? It has no doubt brought blessing, but is there more blessing available? I am suggesting that instead of giving "automatically," that you turn it into a weekly opportunity to hear from God.

In this type of house church, there is no rule that you have to tithe. There are very little costs involved as there are no paid leadership; and by meeting in houses, there is little in the way of facility costs. There will be costs for seminars and courses and for things like catered dinners. For example, with Huios House, since we initially met at the New Life Center, we made tax receipted giving available if people felt led to contribute to the expenses, the vision, or missions of the center. This was an option, not an expectation. We don't anticipate taking an offering as automatic part of our regular meeting.

The doors to the Spirit-led life are readily available to all of us and need to be exercised and encouraged. The goal is to become like Jesus who actually walked in the Spirit.

The Huios House Church Model

We have initiated a new church model on a solid foundation. Our goal is focused on the lordship of Jesus and active in attempts to grow in hearing and obeying God. We employ the wisdom and experience of eldership-level Christians to provide an atmosphere where each member is encouraged to participate and valued for their wisdom and gifts.

By encouraging worship, we hope to build God a place where He can manifest His life. By allowing prophetic prayer in our meetings, we seek to give each one opportunity to exercise this gift of the Holy Spirit in the hope that all will be edified. By testing the words of prophecy, we hope to give honor and credence to the word of the

Lord while benefiting believers with an opportunity to express what God has given them.

We want to demonstrate that it is possible to become *huios*. As *huios*, we pray for our community, for healing in our community, and to disciple new believers from the community—to obey all that the Lord Jesus commanded—in the power of the Holy Spirit.

God is able to do exceedingly and abundantly more than we ask or think.

Glossary

Antinomian: Without law, lawless, without authority. The flesh hates the law of God.

Doulos: Servant or slave, does the will of the Father.

Grace: Divine influence, undeserved favor. The empowering presence of God's Spirit that enables us to do the impossible. God's strength and energy given to the humble, dependent on God, that saves them, heals them, and enables them to do the will of God including turning from sin and working miracles.

Huios: Spirit-led, mature son of God, reflects the nature of the Father, goes about doing good, healing all who are oppressed, but is at the same time directed by the Lord. A huios does the works of the Son in the will of the Father by the power of the Holy Spirit.

Justification: When God says, "Not guilty!" It is process that turns one from being a sinner under the wrath of God into someone accepted and adopted by God. The penalty for sin is paid in full by the blood of Jesus. When we first believe in Jesus and confess Him as Lord, we are by faith justified before God—"just if I'd"—never sinned. It is a gift from God. There is a complete change of legal status. This change is so comprehensive and dynamic it is called becoming a new creature or in effect a new species.

Kingdom of God: The realm of God. That which God rules over including the angels. A territory or people ruled by a king, in this case the King of kings. The kingdom of God is essentially **the government or rule of Christ**. Christ in us, the hope of glory, is the Holy Spirit. The kingdom of God is the central theme of the whole Bible.

Kingdom theology: is teaching that emphasizes the centrality of the lordship of Jesus Christ. It points to the Spirit-controlled life. This teaching reveals the true nature of God—that He is sovereign. And the true nature of man—that he needs redemption, and once redeemed can rule with Christ.

Law: Can mean principle, as in, "The law of the Spirit of life has set me free from the law of death." The word law most often refers to the *Torah*, which means teaching or instruction. In other words, law means the teachings of Moses and in particular the moral law of God as summarized in the Ten Commandments. The Ten Commandments are the only words God gave His people that He actually wrote in His own handwriting. They are a transcript of the nature of God and are unchanging and eternal. The law is good, holy, and of great usefulness and benefit to the Christian. Faith upholds the law, and love fulfills the law. It cannot justify one from sin. It simply reveals sin. It reveals our need for Jesus.

Minister: Servant, focus is on what he does; whereas *doulos* focuses on who he is. All are called to be ministers. All must be equipped. Every believer is a minister including young and old, male and female, Jew and Gentile.

New Birth: Process of initially coming under new government. It is an act of God whereby He plants His incorruptible seed into our spirits and we are made alive spiritually. It is an act of man whereby he recognizes the reality of God, accepts or believes the lordship of Jesus by faith, and confesses with his mouth that Jesus is Lord. He turns from the control of sin and enters into the government or kingdom of God. See Justification.

Sanctification: Process of maturing whereby the carnal or flesh nature of the born-again person, Christian, is taken over by the rule of Christ. Some call it the salvation of the soul. Justification is a rather quick process in which a person's spirit is made alive. We are born again or adopted and become children of God (*teknon*). Sanctification is a rather long process when life in our spirit, influences and permeates our souls. Our actions, behaviors, thoughts, and motives are transformed to become reflective of divine influence. We in effect become like Jesus, a mature Son of God (*huios*).

Teknon: Born-again believer, legal child of God but not yet matured. Has the seed of the Father.

Recommended Reading

Hell's Best Kept Secret by Ray Comfort (New Kensington, PA: Whitaker House, 1989).

Pagan Christianity by Frank Viola and George Barna (Carol Stream, IL: Tyndale-BarnaBooks, 2008).

The Messianic Church Arising by Dr. Robert Heidler (Glory of Zion International, 2006).

The Power of Praying in Tongues by Glenn Arekion (Italy: Destiny Image Europe, 2010).

The Ultimate Treasure Hunt by Kevin Dedmon (Shippensburg, PA: Destiny Image Publishing, 2007).

Truth to Tell by David Pawson (London: Hodder and Soughton, 1993).

Contact the Author

Ian Wilkinson

New Life Centre
28 216 Three Sisters Drive
Canmore, Alberta, Canada T1W 2M2

ianwilk@shaw.ca

Additional copies of this book and other book
titles from EVANGELISTA MEDIA™
and DESTINY IMAGE™ EUROPE
are available at your local bookstore.

We are adding new titles every month!

To view our complete catalog online, visit us at:
www.evangelistamedia.com

Send a request for a catalog to:

Via della Scafa, 29/14
65013 Città Sant'Angelo (Pe), ITALY
Tel. +39 085 4716623 • Fax +39 085 9090113
info@evangelistamedia.com

"Changing the World, One Book at a Time."™

Are you an author?

Do you have a "today" God-given message?

CONTACT US

We will be happy to review your manuscript
for the possibility of publication:

publisher@evangelistamedia.com
http://www.evangelistamedia.com/pages/AuthorsAppForm.htm